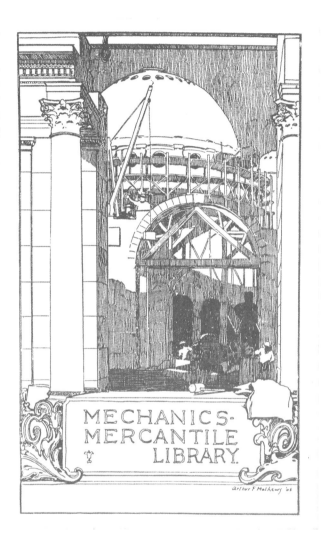

MECHANICS·
MERCANTILE
LIBRARY.

Arthur F. Mathews '06

COMPUTER FORENSICS

COMPUTER FORENSICS

AN ESSENTIAL GUIDE FOR ACCOUNTANTS, LAWYERS, AND MANAGERS

MICHAEL SHEETZ

JOHN WILEY & SONS, INC.

Published by John Wiley & Sons, Inc., Hoboken, New Jersey.
Published simultaneously in Canada.

For general information on our other products and services please contact our Customer Care
Department within the U.S. at 877-762-2974, outside the U.S. at 317-572-3993, or fax 317-572-4002.

Wiley also publishes its books in a variety of electronic formats. Some content that appears in print,
however, may not be available in electronic format.

For more information about Wiley products, visit our Web site at http://www.wiley.com.

Library of Congress Cataloging-in-Publication Data:

Sheetz, Michael.
    Computer forensics : an essential guide for accountants, lawyers, and managers / Michael Sheetz.
        p. cm.
    Includes index.
    ISBN: 978-0-471-78932-1 (cloth)
    1. Computer crimes–Investigation. I. Title.
    HV8079.C65S44 2007
    363.25–dc22

                                                                            2006030331

Printed in the United States of America.

10 9 8 7 6 5 4 3 2 1

This book is dedicated to my mother and father, whose love and encouragement have given me the confidence to dare to dream, and to the memory of my grandfather, Benjamin Franklin Sheetz. His love of the written word lives on in me.

CONTENTS

INTRODUCTION

In today's world, few areas of our lives remain untouched by high-tech gadgets and computers. From our automobiles to the ubiquity of e-mail, the world of bits and bytes has overtaken every phase of our lives. While this ceaseless march of the tide of technology has brought wonderful benefits, as with all gains humankind has experienced, it also has brought some side effects.

Although our efficiency has increased, so have the demands for our time. Not only must we learn to multitask, but we must be available 24 hours a day. Tethered to our cell phones, personal digital assistants, and palm-top computers with twenty-first-century umbilical cords, loved ones and coworkers alike experience withdrawal symptoms and panic attacks if their calls and e-mails remain unanswered for more than 10 minutes.

Arguably nowhere has this technological onslaught had a greater impact than in the business world. E-mail, the World Wide Web, and corporate intranets have insinuated themselves into nearly every business. From the mom-and-pop market, which has a digital storefront to augment its brick-and-mortar operation, to the Fortune 500 multinational whose communications hub depends on the infrastructure of the network we call the Internet, digital traffic directs our lives—occasionally into unsightly rush-hour snarls.

For the average person, the pervasiveness of computers and digital technology is little more than either a convenience or an inconvenience, depending on which side of the digital fence you sit. For others, such as managers, accountants, and lawyers, digital technology signifies much more than that; it signifies a change in the way we look at information.

The "paperless office" and "electronic discovery" are only two of the many phrases that have arisen with the growth of computers, and both bring with them some very serious managerial problems. For the manager seeking to streamline and reduce costs, the paperless office might, at first glance, seem like the ideal solution to growing storage problems. Likewise, electronic discovery and the instantaneous exchange of digital evidence sound like every lawyers' dream—at least at first blush. In reality, hidden difficulties in both areas can blindside professionals and result in tremendously higher costs.

These hidden costs, the land mines of the information age, while mere speed bumps to some, are career-ending hurdles for others. What separates the two is the knowledge of the abilities and limitations of the medium. As an example, let us examine the manager who is weighing the decision to go paperless. On the plus side, there are the obvious benefits of reduced storage space, decreased access time, and, depending on implementation methodology, reduced clerical staff. However, the digitally uninitiated may have overlooked the risks involved.

One very serious risk is security. While access to paper documents such as credit memos and invoices in the traditional office is most often restricted by walls, doors, and metal filing cabinets, the cyberworld lacks those conventional security devices. Instead, things such as firewalls, passwords, and encryption technology stand in the way of unauthorized access. Both methods can be equally secure, and both are vulnerable in their own particular ways. However, most managers understand the weaknesses and vulnerabilities of their physical security assets. Many do not have the same fundamental understanding of the limitations of the digital equivalent.

For the attorney, the situation is similar. In a traditional plaintiff's personal injury firm, many cases follow similar schedules and proceed along the same path. One of the steps in this path is the discovery phase. Discovery is essentially where both sides learn as much about the opponent's case as possible. While at first a counterintuitive concept in an adversarial legal system, the underlying rationale of truth seeking ultimately is supported by the put-your-cards-on-the-table process.

At its heart, the discovery process involves the exchange of information by both sides. In the early days of electronic discovery (e-discovery), electronic communications wrought havoc on some firms—in part due to both the lawyer's and the client's lack of an understanding of the technology. Some of these difficulties centered on the interoffice memo. In the traditional office, memos circulate, get filed, and may ultimately get shredded. This is not necessarily the case in a paperless environment.

Misunderstanding the permanence of e-mail memos, many firms overlooked the persistent existence of such communications on corporate servers, company Web sites, and even employee desktops. More than one case was doomed by the existence of the "smoking gun" memo in electronic form somewhere on the client's computer infrastructure.

As e-discovery became more common, a second issue emerged: information overload. Depending on the case, demands for production can constitute a sizable portion of the discovery process. In a demand for production, one side, usually the plaintiff's, will demand the other side produce evidence, usually documents, that tend to support its theory of the case. In traditional practice, things such as memos, correspondence, personnel evaluations, and the like were photocopied and turned over the demanding party. As you might imagine, the manpower necessary to fulfill such a request can be substantial.

In the paperless environment, it might appear that the response to the same demand would be a simple matter of copying the electronic documents to disk, or in a large office a CD, and turning it over, requiring fewer personnel, fewer hours, and less copy cost. Not necessarily. As e-discovery has progressed, many firms, plaintiffs, and defendants have become painfully aware of just how much e-matter can be accumulated by even small and medium-size businesses. Sifting through hundreds of documents and thousands of e-mails to find relevant and nonprotected items that match the request might involve more time than researching and copying the equivalent number of paper-based documents.

Add to this the potential for format incompatibility and costs quickly mount. Unlike paper-based documents, which anyone can read, e-documents are often generated in proprietary formats that are readable only by the system in which they were created. If the requesting party does not have access to the proprietary format, these e-documents might as well be written in invisible ink. This results in greater costs to one or both sides when someone must translate them into a common language. Issues such as who bears the cost burden and what constitutes improper behavior quickly moved to the forefront in the legal practice during the early days of e-discovery.

Everything new that emerges—telephone, automobile, and computer—has gone through various stages of growth and development during which many of the bugs and glitches have been ironed out. This Darwinesque process helps to ensure that only the benefits of the technology remain and the weaknesses are cast to the wayside. Although not entirely successfully, the process allows humans to catch up with the technology, and sometimes results in subsequent generations of products that are far superior to their ancestors.

The evolution of things like the paperless office and e-discovery has been under way for many years. In large part, many of the issues that I have touched on have been addressed, corrected, or at least worked around. Many issues still remain to be examined, however, and as digital technology grows in scope and power, many more will arise. One of the areas that is still often misunderstood is the area of computer forensics.

As a part of the larger field of forensics, computer forensics is lumped together with such interesting fields of study as forensic entomology (bugs and insects), forensic anthropology (study of bones and skeletons), and DNA analysis (a branch of forensic biology). Although sharing some real similarities with its brethren, computer forensics has emerged into a distinct specialty that roams beyond the confines of traditional forensic science.

Rarely, if ever, would forensic scientists in fields such as entomology, odontology, or anthropology consult on cases outside the criminal venue. There are, of course, the occasional personal injury and wrongful death cases requiring such expertise, but by and large, historically forensic scientists are called only in criminal prosecutions. As such, much of the expertise and talent has been developed through state-supported facilities such as crime labs and universities.

The field of computer forensic examination is different. Whether attributable to such media phenomenon as the CSI series or due to the pervasive nature of computer technology, the science of computer forensic examination has exploded onto the scene. With this explosion has also come a tremendous amount of misinformation, and this misinformation can be tremendously costly. You cannot plan properly if you make incorrect assumptions or simply misunderstand the capabilities of the science. Improper planning will ultimately cost money.

The answer is this book. Although I cannot make a computer forensic technician of you, nor do I hope to, I can help you to better understand the potential and limitations of this fascinating field. Many universities now offer entire majors dedicated to the field. Postgraduate dissertations have been undertaken in subfields of this field, and the body of knowledge in this area is so rapidly expanding that by the time this book is on the shelves, new discoveries and techniques will have emerged that I have not included. Therefore, it is not a field manual on how to recover computer forensic evidence. Instead, it is, as the title suggests, a guide.

Computer Forensics: The Essential Guide for Managers, Accountants, and Lawyers is aimed at managers, accountants, and lawyers—and more. Students, parents, and even crime-drama enthusiasts should find something of interest and will find the text free from overly technical discussions of the underlying bits and bytes of the process. Instead, I have decided to focus primarily on the concepts and capabilities of the field—with some technical discussion thrown in. If you find yourself lost or your head is spinning at some places in this book, take heart. You can benefit from this book even if you don't grasp the details of some of our discussions.

Although I would like to think that anyone can benefit from this book, I will caution that it is not intended as a comprehensive guide on computer forensic evidence. I encourage the computer professional to read it, but it does not contain the nuts-and-bolts details of securing, imaging, and analyzing digital evidence that other more technical volumes provide. It is more general and broad than that. As an introduction to the field it will serve well.

As we move forward, I encourage you to explore the suggested reading and delve into areas that you find particularly interesting. I will point you in the right direction and offer you as much insight as possible. Where you go from there is entirely up to you.

ACKNOWLEDGMENTS

I would like to acknowledge Preston Mighdol, Chief of the Palm Beach County State Attorney's Economic Crime Division, for his guidance and suggestions over the years. I would also like to thank my colleague Dr. Grace Telesco, whose patient counsel and insightful advice helped shape this book immeasurably.

COMPUTER FORENSICS

A Definition of Computer Forensics

INTRODUCTION

In this chapter, I introduce the science of computer forensics—both what it is and what it is not. Although the term is heard these days with increasing frequency, the discipline itself has existed for only a short time. Only within the past 20 years has the admission of digital evidence gained consistent recognition in our court systems. In fact, some courts systems around the world may not admit certain types of digital evidence. As you might imagine, given the relative youth of this area of study, some mistakes were made early on. It is to be hoped that those mistakes have been long since corrected, and, while completely smooth sailing is doubtful, at least calmer seas are on the horizon. As we begin this journey, it is only fitting to lay some groundwork. This groundwork, in the form of history, will help provide a clearer picture of the role that computer forensics plays in our legal system. It begins with a discussion of forensics itself.

FORENSIC SCIENCE

The term "forensics" is often misunderstood and is frequently misused. Whether in popular television or the news media, the term is often thrown around without regard to what it actually means. From the Latin *forensis*, the term means "belonging to, used in or suitable to courts of judicature or to public discussion and debate."[1] Forensics exists independently of any particular field of study.

For example, forensic entomology, while grouped with other forensic fields, is really nothing more than the scientific study of insects, with the added qualifier that it is done with a goal of introduction into court. In fact, Gil Grissom of television's *CSI* is probably America's most famous forensic entomologist, albeit a fictional one, and has single-handedly made bug lovers sexy.

In reality, although there are a small group of fields in which forensic analysis is common, practically any field of study is amenable to such work. For example, most people have heard of forensic psychologists, who offer evidence in court regarding mental states and conditions; few people know that there are forensic engineers, who offer scientific evidence within their subspecialty. For example, a forensic electrical engineer might offer testimony regarding the cause of a fire related to faulty wiring. Fewer people still have heard of the field of forensic linguistics. Since linguistics is the study of language, a forensic linguist might be used to analyze the language used in a suicide note, compared to miscellaneous writings of the deceased prior to death, to try to determine if the note was in fact written by the deceased.

Therefore, by extension of this logic, computer forensics is the scientific study of computers in a manner consistent with the principles of the rules of evidence and court rules of procedure. This is exactly what the field of computer forensics is. It is also important to understand what it is not.

Even among those knowledgeable in the field, some confusion exists over what particular areas of computer science should actually be included under the umbrella of computer forensics. In order to better illustrate what is, and what is not, traditionally considered computer forensics, a brief history of the evolution of computer science into the study of computer forensics is helpful.

HISTORY OF COMPUTER FORENSICS

The most influential aspects of computer history are the history of the machines themselves. The evolution of the computer from a mysterious black box of interest only to academics and technical types, to a ubiquitous fixture in nearly every home, is a unique and interesting story.

Once of the biggest changes to occur is the sheer size of the computer. In the early 1950's the first computers were housed in buildings dedicated solely to their operation. These behemoths, less sophisticated than today's three-dollar calculator, were unbelievably costly and amazingly temperamental. Designed and built using conventional vacuum tubes, many of the circuits were large enough for computer scientists to actually walk among the components removing debris and small bugs that were causing malfunctions—hence the term "bug," which in computer lingo signifies an operating glitch. Their size and cost made the first computers little more than curiosities for the average American. In fact, until 1981, when IBM released its first personal computer (PC), personal home computers were a rarity.[2]

Or perhaps the mystique that shrouds the computer is the result of the fact that computers speak their own language. Originally computers were nonprogrammable in the sense we think of today. Eventually, as they evolved, the ability to change their configuration emerged, and while difficult under the best conditions, changes could be made to their functionality. As the power of the computational ability of computers expanded during the late 1940s and 1950s, interacting with the computers became a greater focus.

In 1954 John Backus, an employee of IBM, developed the first high-level programming language.[3] This language, FORTRAN, short for formula translation, was subsequently released commercially, and thus began the computer revolution. Prior to FORTRAN and other high-level languages that would follow, such as COBOL and C++, the only way to communicate with the computer was through machine language: a series of 0s and 1s. Machine language eventually led to a second layer of language known as assembly language, which turned the 0s and 1s of machine code into human words, such as PUSH, POP, and MOVE.

From this highly complicated language system emerged FORTRAN and COBOL and later C+. These high-level languages, while much simpler than machine language, were still well beyond the capabilities and comprehension of the average citizen, which contributed to the mystique of computers. Unlike the telephone, which was an unprecedented phenomenal scientific advancement in its own right, you needed to know an entirely new language to communicate with computers.

Whatever the reason, whether cost or communication barriers, computers remained an academic and military phenomenon for much of their early lives. However, as computers began to take a foothold, a cottage industry of home computer kits emerged. These kits, ranging in cost from $1,500 to $4000, were targeted to computer and electronics hobbyists who wanted to own their own computer—some assembly required.[4]

Historically, many of the advances in the home computer, later rebranded the personal computer thanks to IBM's marketing of the IBM-PC, occurred in a hobbyist, garage-tinkering way. Industry leaders such as Bill Gates, Steve Jobs, and Steve Wozniak began their careers by building home-brewed versions of commercial products. Were it not for the innovations of these early pioneers, the PC would not have evolved in the fashion it had.[5] This characteristic is much more than an interesting footnote to history. On the contrary, I believe it is the single most important factor influencing the nature of computer forensics.

The modality through which early home computers evolved promoted an environment of innovation and tinkering, the heart and soul of which is exploration and adaptation. I liken the environment of the 1970s and early 1980s, during which some of the greatest advancements in home computers were made, to a young child disassembling a parent's transistor radio to figure out how it works. This spirit of exploration, while at the heart of most all innovations and inventions, would have been no different from the exploration of our ancestors such as Guglielmo Marconi and Enrico Fermi, but for the influence of one phenomenon: the Internet.

There is some disagreement over the actual origin of the Internet. Some claim that it was built in cooperation with the Department of Defense as a vast nationwide "communications bomb shelter." Others argue that it was more about linking research institutions together than providing for the common defense.[6] Regardless of which side you believe, the Internet was in fact originally a small network of computers known as the ARPANET. The ARPANET originally consisted of four computers located at research facilities at the University of California at Los Angeles, Stanford, the University of California at Santa Barbara, and the University of Utah. From those humble beginnings there arose the phenomenon we know today.[7]

Much like the PC, the environment in which the ARPANET began to grow greatly influenced its development. From its early days, the Internet began to evolve as a space for the exchange of information—a common, if you will, where both ideas and academic materials could flow freely. This flow of information was in fact so freely flowing that as the network began to grow, so did military concerns for security. After more and more nonmilitary institutions began joining the network, the Department of Defense decided to abandon it in favor of its own network. In 1983 MILnet was formed using the same basic backbone of the original system.[8]

It was from this original academic mind-set that the Internet as we know it emerged. Understanding the academic background of the Internet is important because of the type of community that it promoted among its users. This community was formed in the spirit of cooperation and free sharing of information. Academic pursuit thrives on knowledge and information and the free flow of ideas and unfettered access. In the early days, the concept of ownership and regulation of this "cyber" space were the last things on the minds of the newly emerging netizens. In this almost "Wild West frontier" environment, the rules, such as they were, were loose, highly fluid, and designed as honor codes more than traditional rules. Information and free access were king and queen, and citizens of this new domain were short on regulation and long on enthusiasm.[9]

This attitude coupled with the developments in the PC world created the beginnings of our computer forensic industry. Computer icons like Bill Gates, Steve Jobs, and Steven Wozniak built their fortunes on more than merely the spirit of competition. They built them on innovation born of the spirit of exploration and tinkering and a how-can-I-make-it-better attitude. The Internet in its early days of nonregulation was an environment tailor made for this entrepreneurial spirit. Additionally, the average computer user during the early days of the Internet was more like Bill Gates than today's black-box user.

Computers were more a phenomenon of the hobbyist and electronics buff than a fixture in every home. As a result, these users shared much more closely the personality traits of the early adopters like Gates, Wozniak, and Jobs. All these traits—openness, innovation, and exploration—combined to create a free-wheeling world in which the only rules were that there were really no rules.

WORLD WIDE WEB

For some readers not old enough to remember, there was a day in which the Internet was not the World Wide Web. Although those two terms are often used interchangeably, they are in fact two different concepts. The Internet, as I explained, is the network infrastructure upon which the communications between linked nodes traverse. The World Wide Web is the linked set of the pages that make up each site on the Internet. In a way very similar to the impact that the graphical user interface (GUI) had on the PC, the development of hypertext markup language (HTML) revolutionized the Internet.

Prior to HTML, the Internet was in use by scientists, academic types, and serious hobbyists with a strong technical grounding. However, the rest of us were still living in the real world, not the cyberworld. The reason for this is again language.

Prior to the adoption of HTML, Internet communication was done through typed commands and very technical instructions. The most prevalent language at that time was a form of the high-level programming language known as UNIX. While a very powerful language, and the origin of many subsequent languages, such as C and C++, UNIX requires memorization of often confusing keywords that must be typed, precisely, on a blank screen. One misspelled word and the command is rejected. This was no different from the state of personal computers under the Disk Operating System (DOS) and Control/Program Monitor (CP/M) operating systems. The GUI changed this.

The GUI, first introduced in the Lisa computer introduced by Apple, made the functionality of the computer independent from the user's knowledge of computer commands.[10] Point and click, drag and drop, and iconic selection were born and in turn gave birth to the World Wide Web revolution. The GUI made the average user, without the slightest knowledge of computer language, a computer genius.

HTML became the GUI of the Internet. By presenting users with pictures, buttons, and tabs from which to choose, programmers removed the requirement of well-developed computer knowledge. Computer access for the masses was born. However, just because the revolution was in progress does not mean that UNIX and the way of the computer guru had disappeared. It was in this environment, on the cusp of the Internet revolution, that I first had a chance to encounter the computer counterculture.

HACKER COMMUNITY

My first encounter with hacking can be instructive in that it illustrates how computer forensics has evolved from intrusion detection and why the two are entirely different areas with entirely different goals.

In the "old days," circa 1990, while working as a criminal investigator, I was introduced to two young boys roughly 15 years old. They were not yet old enough to drive but were quite computer literate. A road patrol officer dropped them at my desk explaining they had been caught prowling around the bushes in a middle-class neighborhood. In their backpacks officers found a stack of computer paper (the old perforated continuous-form kind), a spiral notebook, a flashlight, and an orange lineman's handset (the sort of handheld telephone receiver with alligator clip connectors that telephone repairmen use to test lines). Unsure of what crime they might be committing, but sure they were up to no good nonetheless, they brought them to me. Not because I was the high-tech detective, but because I happened to have the misfortune of being the first in the office.

After an unproductive series of grunts and smirks and a final "I've got nothing to say," they were both released to their parents with juvenile referrals for loitering and prowling. Their backpack remained behind.

An inventory of its contents would send me into a new world, one in which I would spend a large portion of the rest of my career. The purpose of the flashlight was clear; the purpose of the rest of the contents, not so much.

The computer printout could just as easily have been in a foreign language, and the lineman's handset, while I was familiar with what it does, did not immediately reveal what the boys were up to. What did was the notebook. Within its pages were a list of phone numbers with distant area codes and exotic names. Research revealed that these names and phone numbers were for computer bulletin board systems (BBSs). These bulletin boards were the forerunner to today's Internet, and were private sites to which callers could connect through dial-up modems.

Before the days of the Internet and World Wide Web, the only way to connect from site to site was through a direct-dialed connection. While fairly simple in theory, in practice this became a very time-consuming—and expensive—undertaking. At that time, cell phones were a speck on the horizon, and the days of unlimited calling were unheard of. In order to connect to a BBS in a distant area code, the caller would incur long-distance charges. Add to that the technology bottleneck of a modem operating at 28.8 Kbps (kilobits per second; compared to the average speed of 6 to 8 Mbps [megabits per second] for today's Digital Subscriber Lines (DSL) and cable modems, and phone bills in the range of thousands of dollars were common.

What possible reason would someone risk an exorbitantly high phone bill in order to connect to a distant computer? Besides child pornography (which was as popular then as it is today), computer hacking. The two boys in my office were computer hackers who, armed with a list of hacker Web sites, were downloading small program excerpts known as exploits that would help them break into computers. In addition to exploits, the BBSs provided tutorials, computer manuals on most large mainframe computer systems, and an assortment of tools to equip the well-armed hacker.

For me, this was an eye-opening experience. It began me on my journey, a journey in which I would learn about a community that operated by a different set of rules, a set of rules that set the stage for all that would follow in the computer forensic world.

At that time, computer hackers subscribed to a code known as the "Hacker Manifesto," a pithy rebellious explanation or, more accurately, a rationalization for what they do. This page-long diatribe allegedly written in 1986 by a hacker named "The Mentor" blames a society of adults for the angst of the teen and uses this as justification for their knowledge-seeking behavior. The credo was written shortly after his arrest in 1986 and first appeared the hacker underground newspaper *Phrack*. The final few paragraphs of this credo are particularly appropriate:

> *This is our world now . . . the world of the electron and the switch, the beauty of the baud. We make use of a service already existing without paying for what could be dirt-cheap if it wasn't run by profiteering gluttons, and you call us criminals. We explore . . . and you call us criminals. We seek after knowledge . . . and you call us criminals. We exist without skin color, without nationality, without religious bias . . . and you call us criminals. You build atomic bombs, you wage wars, you murder, cheat, and lie to us and try to make us believe it's for our own good, yet we're the criminals.*
>
> *Yes, I am a criminal. My crime is that of curiosity. My crime is that of judging people by what they say and think, not what they look like. My crime is that of outsmarting you, something that you will never forgive me for.*
>
> *I am a hacker, and this is my manifesto. You may stop this individual, but you can't stop us all . . . after all, we're all alike.*[11]

The Mentor, who was later identified as Loyd Blankenship, was a member of an underground hacking group known as the Legion of Doom, believed by some to be the largest and best-organized of the hacker groups in the 1980s. Their attitude is typical of the attitude of the hacker community during that time.[12]

I use the term "community" purposely, since during that time the way of thinking was very much a community of us versus them: hacker versus nonhacker. The manifesto's stated goal of knowledge seeking and exploration probably hit its most fevered pitch during the Great Hacker War. While the title seems melodramatic, the competition that raged between the Legion of Doom and its rival faction, Masters of Deception, during a brief period during the early 1990s was driven by the goal of gaining entry to computers for the sake of prestige within the community.

Knowledge seeking, as you may recall, fits in well with the personality of the computer entrepreneur and the Internet founders. My introduction to this mind-set in the "Hacker Manifesto" ultimately led me to seek information from the mainstream computer community.

At that time, PCs were not yet household items. Although most major universities offered courses in computer science, computers were still something of an oddity in the home. Mainframe computers, however, were well established, so I turned to a number of local computer professionals. With their guidance, I learned my second essential lesson: Computer professionals were more concerned with protection than prosecution. At first, this distinction may sound negligible, but in the context of the evolution of computer evidence, it proves to be a key element.

The prevailing mind-set was to identify the vulnerability, patch the hole, and kick intruders off the system. For most if not all system administrators (to the extent that that position even existed back then), this approach was necessitated for two reasons.

First, when dealing with a large company, the admission that a hacker compromised the system would be extremely damaging to the public image. We see this even today. By admitting that a system has been hacked, the business admits that it has failed to protect customer assets. In many cases, the loss of revenue due to the admission is far greater than the cost of simply plugging the hole and moving on.

Second, many viewed the intrusion as an inconvenience, not a crime. It is helpful to keep in mind that many of the information technology (IT) professionals in system administrator positions share a common bond with the hacker community: shared inquisitiveness. As a result, many system administrators saw intrusions, especially where nothing was stolen or damaged, as more prank than grounds for prosecution.

In this atmosphere, there was very little room for concern over things like the admissibility of evidence and chain of custody. Administrators were both ignorant of and complacent about the rules of evidence and the need to secure a conviction. As I mentioned, their concern was a secure system. To the extent that administrators began asking for police assistance, most of the time it was done after the fact, and after, as we discuss in later chapters, valuable evidentiary data had been destroyed.

In this atmosphere, by the time police were called, the law enforcement response suffered from an overwhelming lack of knowledge, which manifested itself on several levels. First, during this era, most police agencies, even large ones, had no one trained to recognize or investigate computer crimes. It was not until computer crime began gaining more media attention that police departments began identifying and training investigators in the unique demands of computer investigations. Even today, a number of small and medium-size agencies do not maintain a full-time high-tech crime unit, and a handful still fail to routinely train officers in digital evidence recovery. These agencies ignore the fact that recovering digital evidence differs in some substantial ways from recovering nondigital evidence.

At another level, the public response was lacking. By this I mean that the system itself—our criminal justice system—was ill-prepared to handle and prosecute these types of offenders. For example, during the early years of the rise in computer-based crime, laws for dealing with the unique elements comprising a computer crime were often ineffective. As a result, prosecutions were often impossible because, by law, the suspect's conduct was not "illegal." Fortunately, since that time, all states have addressed this issue, and fairly uniform laws are in place nationwide and federally to deal effectively with all types of computer crimes.

Finally, since computer evidence recovery was in its infancy, there were no established and documented procedures in place. Although the general rules of evidence offered guidance, a lack of knowledge about the nature of digital evidence made the application of the rules very difficult. In short, we were learning as we went, and in doing so, the only model we had for use was the model of the computer professional: a nonlegal model. Adding to this lack of knowledge was the fact that those from whom we could seek legal guidance were equally clueless regarding the true nature of digital evidence. These factors made early evidence collection methods highly suspect by today's standards.

Fortunately, as we have moved forward, our knowledge of digital evidence and of the role the computer professional plays in its recovery has improved vastly. It is the role that the computer professional plays that brings me to my conclusion that intrusion detection, while perhaps a subfield of computer forensics, is essentially not a forensic field.

Experts in the area of intrusion detection can, and often should, think like computer forensic technicians; however, many of the things that intrusion detection requires are not necessarily compatible with the best practices of forensic recovery. For example, tracking down and kicking out an intruder to a system will, by its very nature, require the alteration of digital evidence. The alteration of digital evidence is something that forensic technicians must protect against in order to establish reliability of the evidence. Therefore, the actions of a system administrator who identifies an intruder and subsequently deletes the Trojan horse or exploit that was planted to gain superuser access will compromise future ability to prosecute the intruder. Likewise, in some cases collecting the evidence necessary to prosecute the intruder may reduce the system administrator's ability to protect the system, at least in the short term. In the end, both approaches require a compromise. Succeeding with both roles simultaneously is not impossible; it does require, however, that both jobs recognize the limitations and demands of the other.

CONCLUSION

As you can see, my earlier statement that intrusion detection and computer forensics have different goals is correct. Because I see the role of the intrusion detection profession as different from the role of the computer forensic professional, I would categorize them separately, and do not consider intrusion detection under the broad umbrella of computer forensics. Ultimately it will be up to you to decide, and if you are an IT professional or direct an IT staff, on occasion you may be faced with the dilemma of having to choose between those two goals. As we move into the next chapter, bear in mind the brief history that we have covered here. While far from comprehensive, it should help you to understand better the direction we may be headed.

In the next chapter, we begin our discussion of exactly what computer forensics entails and get to know the components and processes of a computer system. As always, remember that this is not a how-to manual or a reference source on collecting digital evidence but an introduction to the field of computer forensics and its limitations.

NOTES

1. *Webster's New Universal Unabridged Dictionary,* 2nd ed. (New York: Barnes & Noble Books, 2003).
2. See generally Paul E. Cerruzzi, *The History of Modern Computing,* 2nd ed. (Cambridge, MA: MIT Press, 2003).
3. IBM Archives, "John Backus," www-03.ibm.com/ibm/history/exhibits/builders/builders_backus.html.
4. See generally Christos J. P. Moschovitis, Hilary Poole, Tami Schuyler, and Theresa M. Senft, *History of the Internet: A Chronology, 1843 to Present* (Santa Barbara, CA: ABC-CLIO, 1999). See also Mary Bellis, "The First Hobby and Home Computers: Scelbi, Mark-8, Altair, IBM 5100," Inventors of the Modern Computer, http://inventors.about.com/library/weekly/aa120198.htm
5. Ibid.
6. Moschovitis et al., *History of the Internet,* pp. 52–55; See also Bellis, "ARPANET—The First Internet," Inventors of the Modern Computer, http://inventors.about.com/ library/ weekly/aa091598.htm.
7. Moschovitis et al., *History of the Internet.*
8. Ibid.
9. See generally Lawrence Lessig, *Code and Other Laws of Cyberspace* (New York: Basic Books, 1999).
10. Mary Bellis, "The History of the Graphical User Interface," Inventors of the Modern Computer, http://inventors. about.com/library/weekly/aa043099.htm.
11. The Mentor, "The Conscience of a Hacker," *Phrack, Inc.* 1, no. 7 (1986); available at: http://www.phrack.org/phrack/7/P07–03.

12. Bernadette H. Schell and John L. Dodge, *The Hacking of America* (Westport, CT: Quorum Books, 2002), p. 123. See also *Wikipedia, The Free Encyclopedia,* http://en.wikipedia.org/w/index.php?title=Loyd_ Blankenship&oldid=76258023.

SUGGESTED READING

Levy, Steven. *Hackers: Heroes of the Computer Revolution*. New York: Penguin Books, 1994.

Slatalla, Michelle. *The Masters of Deception: The Gang that Ruled Cyberspace*. London: Harper-Perennial, 1996.

2

BASICS OF COMPUTER FORENSIC CONCEPTS

INTRODUCTION

As discussed briefly in Chapter 1, the goal of computer forensics is the recovery of evidence for use in court. Whether the case is civil or criminal, the same basic sets of evidentiary rules are in play. Foremost among these rules are the rules of admissibility, which I discuss in greater detail in later chapters. The goal of the forensic computer examiner is to obtain evidence in a legally admissible way. This chapter focuses on the basic principles that underlie the digital evidence collection process.

It is important to keep in mind that the collection of digital evidence often requires quick thinking and adaptability. Therefore, the steps outlined in later chapters are only a basic guide to understanding the flow of the process.

Steps taken during the preservation stage can be the key to successful evidence recovery. None of the steps in the process should be thought of as more or less important than the others, and it is crucial to think of them as equal parts of a complicated process. However, the preservation stage is often the one most likely to doom a case. In order to provide the best opportunity to succeed, computer technicians must remember that digital evidence is unlike all other forms of evidence. Digital evidence is highly volatile. In reality, digital evidence is nothing more than a series of electronic impulses stored in more or less stable form. These stored impulses *are* the evidence; once they change, the evidence is destroyed.

Conversely, things such as records, documents, and photographs are relatively stable. Barring some major event, records and documents remain fairly unchanged over time. To understand why digital evidence is so different, you must understand the nature of digital evidence in the first place.

UNDERSTANDING DIGITAL EVIDENCE

Understanding how computers process information and relate to the outside world is important in any discussion of computer forensics. Regardless of your goal—whether it is to become a computer forensic technician or simply to have a better understanding of the forensic process—you must understand how computers operate. Obviously for technicians, the level of knowledge in this area must be much higher. Because this text is not written with technicians in mind, I only offer the broad-stroke overview. Even readers with zero or little computer knowledge should have no trouble following along. Experienced computer users may consider skipping forward; however, a little refresher never hurt anyone. This section begins with a discussion of computer systems in general and then moves to the more complicated areas of data storage.

As we continue, I want you to expand your concept of a computer. While large boxy machines perched on our desktops are the quintessential computer we all think of, computers in today's world take on any variety of forms, from MP3 music players, to cellular phones, to automobiles. Hardly a component of our daily lives is not a computer or touched by one. For computer forensic professionals, this expanded definition makes investigation and recovery that much more difficult because of the influence of proprietary technology.

Every computer, no matter how simple or complicated, can be broken down into four basic components: input, storage, processing, and output.

Input allows the user in the real-world to interact with the computer. Input devices, such as keyboards, mice, and pen tablets, are all forms of input devices. Storage is comprised of both permanent and temporary devices such as hard drives, RAM (random access memory), and flash drives. The purpose of storage is to hold data for later retrieval by the processing component. The processing component manipulates the data based on the instructions it is given. Examples of the processing unit are the central processing unit (CPU) of the computer, other ancillary processors such as graphics processing units (GPUs) on some graphics cards, and firmware that controls disks or printers, for example. Output devices are necessary for the computer to reveal the results of the processing to the outside world. Obvious examples of output devices are monitors and printers.

As with all oversimplifications, there are some areas of overlap: The touch screen monitor, for instance, functions as an input and output device, and more complex system hybrids can be found. Essentially, however, the listed components are present on most any functioning computer system.

INPUT

Input devices come in a nearly endless variety. Depending on the application, they can range from a simple mouse, to a keyboard, to a $15,000 three-dimensional scanner. All input devices, however, share one common characteristic: They take information from the outside world and feed it into the computer's storage.

Although computers have come a long way since the early 1930s, when they were first conceived, they cannot yet read the minds of their users. To solve this problem, keyboards allow us to translate our typed thoughts into something the computer can comprehend. Depending on the process and the input device, the user input may be converted into machine-readable information while it is input or may be passed into some sort of processing unit for translation. Regardless of the method, typing the letter a on the keyboard results in the binary equivalent of that character in memory for use by the processing unit.

STORAGE

Storage is an important concept for the computer investigator because the majority of the evidence that will be recovered during the investigation will come directly from the computer's storage system. Whether the storage system is a hard disk, compact disc (CD), digital video disc (DVD), or perhaps the system random access memory (RAM), the information that is of interest to the investigation will be there. Most people immediately think of the hard drive as the primary source of stored information, but system RAM is also tremendously valuable. For example, while doing a live analysis, which will be discussed in Chapter 8, the information contained in RAM is very important. But investigators must be careful, because once removed, RAM is gone forever.

In addition, analysis of embedded systems, such as cellular phones, and MP3 players, such as iPods, requires that you recognize the potential for storage of evidence. An iPod is a perfect example of an often-overlooked storage asset. Although the iPod traditionally is used as a music playback system, it is nothing more than a small computer with a nearly 40-gigabyte (GB) hard drive embedded in it. Considering the entire text of the manuscript of this book could easily fit on a 700-megabyte (MB) CD hundreds of times (1 GB equals roughly 1,000 MB), you can imagine the wealth of information you can find on a single iPod if you know where to look.

PROCESSING

Once the information has been input to storage, the processing unit takes over. In reality, the processing unit has been involved from the beginning. In fact, depending on the speed of the computer and the nature of the task, the processing may be accomplished prior to storage in volatile memory. However, for the purpose of this discussion, we will assume that the first stop of the data is in storage.

The processor is the heart of the machine, and more or less controls the operation of the other peripheral components. Depending on the type of device and its role in the investigation, the original processing unit may be fairly insignificant. For example, most forensic analyses will be done on a machine other than the machine on which the data was first collected and manipulated. The investigator may access the target machine to secure and collect the digital evidence, but most likely the evidence will be examined on a different machine in the controlled environment of the computer lab. This makes the particular processor of the target machine fairly inconsequential.

Regardless of how important the processing unit is to the investigation, because it is the heart of the system, it is crucial to understand how it operates. Processor types vary widely in their capabilities and functions. The processors most people are familiar with are the processors at the heart of the personal computer (PC) and the Apple systems. These are far and away the most popular processors in desktop and laptop personal computers, but they are not the only choices. Therefore, instead of talking about an Intel Pentium 4 or an old MC68000, I will focus on how processors handle data in general. In order to better understand that, it is important to understand computer data generally.

WHAT COMPUTER DATA IS

Most people are familiar with the fact that computers operate on a binary system, but few really understand what that means. None of us really believes that our word processing document, in its original form, is sitting on our hard drive somewhere, but most of us do not consider what form it actually takes or how it gets there in the first place. Even though the intricacies of how the logic processors of the CPU manipulate the registers which are merely temporary storage devices and perform arithmetic calculations on memory addresses are far beyond the scope of this book, it is important to cover the basics. It is especially important to understand how a computer program relates to operating systems such as Windows, since these programs do many things "behind the scenes" that will ruin evidence and potentially destroy a case.

Computer data, regardless of where it came from or where it is going, is stored in binary form in the storage device. To better understand what binary data is, we must also understand the difference between digital and analog. Analog signals are signals that have an infinitely varying value between two points. An example is an electric current that varies between +1 and −1 volts. As the current strength varies between those two poles, it passes through each possible value between −1 and +1. Since there are an infinite number of values between those points, the signal is infinitely variable.

One of the most popular examples of an analog process is a tape recording. When a musical signal is recorded to tape in analog form, the complete infinitely varying signal is transformed in to electrical impulses and faithfully recorded on the magnetic surface of the tape in one very smooth, undulating curve. All the variations of the signal are captured. Another example of an analog waveform is a trumpet playing a musical note. The musical note, which has a frequency dependent on its pitch, is a continuous waveform with an amplitude and frequency specific to its pitch and volume. If it helps, envision the typical sine wave from your high school trigonometry book. These waves represent all possible values between to points.

Conversely, digital signals have two states: on and off. In the digital world, we represent "on" with the number 1 and "off" with 0. Conveniently, the binary number system, which has only two digits, can assist. In the binary number system 0 and 1 perfectly match our digital signal. Compared to the decimal system's digits 0 through 9, the fewer digits of the binary system may at first appear to be a limitation. It is not.

In fact, even though the nine digits of the decimal system offer more possibilities than the binary system, there are still limitations. In the decimal system, what happens when you count above 9? The answer is simply to move one column to the left, add a digit, and begin with 0 once again—9 plus 1 is 0 and carry the 1 to the next column. This simple trick we all learned in third grade works no differently in the binary system. Conversion is a fairly simple matter.

Because we can represent any number or combination of numbers in binary format, we can use a series of 0s and 1s (offs and ons) to store any information. Depending on what we want to store, this becomes more or less complicated.

If we want to store numerical data in the computer, we simply convert the number into binary. For example, to store the number 7,345, we would encode that as binary 1110010110001, ultimately storing that series of digits in memory as either ons or offs.

The example of the numbers is pretty straightforward. Storing word processing documents and photographs is more difficult. Once we know how to do it, it is fairly easy to convert decimal numbers to binary numbers. But what about letters? In most computer applications, such as word processors, spreadsheets, databases, and other higher-level programs, numbers are treated as if they were characters. Therefore, the simple decimal-to-binary conversion does not occur. Since letters and numbers treated as characters, which have no direct binary equivalent, we must find some other way of representing them. Enter the American Standard Code for Information Exchange (ASCII).

ASCII (pronounced ask key) is a code that allows translation of alphanumeric characters between different computer systems.[1] It does this by assigning each alphanumeric character a number between 0 and 127. That number is then converted to binary for storage in the computer. Since there are only 51 alpha characters (upper and lower case) and 10 digits, that leaves 66 remaining ASCII numbers, which are used to store punctuation and special control characters, such as carriage returns and formatting marks.

Although this system of representing all numbers in binary and ASCII is easy for a computer, it can be very difficult for humans. To make things somewhat simpler for humans, the system of hexadecimal (or hex) notation

Base 10	0–9	10	11	12	13	14	15
Base 16	0–9	A	B	C	D	E	F

EXHIBIT 2.1 EXAMPLE OF HEXADECIMAL NOTATION

was adopted. Hexadecimal notation is based on a system of 16 digits, which is called base-16.

Understanding hex is not as difficult as it may first sound. In our decimal system, known as base-10, we use the numerals 0 to 9 to represent all possible values. In hex, we use the numerals 0 to 9, but since that is only 10 possible values and we need 16 for our system, we add the letters A to F; mapping the base-10 system into the base-16 works as shown in Exhibit 2.1.

Hexadecimal notation is nothing more than a system of counting by 16. Just like our more familiar base-10 system and the less familiar base-2 (binary), base-16 can be used to represent an infinite number of values. The advantage of base-16 over base-2 is that hexadecimal can represent, using only two digits, a number that requires eight digits in base-2.

For example, the numbers shown in Exhibit 2.2 all represent the same value.

As illustrated, a value that requires 16 digits to represent in binary and 5 to represent in base-10 only requires 4 in base-16. A further benefit, and one that experienced computer users quickly master, is the fact that each binary number can be broken down into groups of four, and each of these groups map directly to a hex digit. Exhibit 2.3 should make this point clearer.

One of the advantages of the hexadecimal system is that conversion from base-2 to base-16 is much simpler than conversion to base-10, and conversion from base-16 to base-10 is also much easier than conversion from base-2

Base 10	Base 2	Base 16
58143	1110001100011111	E31F

EXHIBIT 2.2 BASE-10, BASE-2, AND BASE-16 RENDERINGS OF THE SAME NUMBER

Binary	1110	0011	0001	1111
Hex	E	3	1	F

EXHIBIT 2.3 BINARY TO HEX CONVERSION

to base-10. Although computer forensic experts are more comfortable working in hex than in binary, computers cannot actually read hex—remember we have only two choices, 0 and 1. Therefore, forensic professionals use translation programs such as WinHex, which I describe later.

If this all seems rather intimidating, relax; it makes perfect sense to computer forensic experts. Although understanding that conversions occur among these three systems of notation is important, being able to convert or calculate hexadecimal math problems is not necessary. If you wish to move forward in your forensic computer education, you will internalize these three different systems and before long will be able to add hex numbers as easily as you now add base-10 numbers.

Representing photographs is slightly more complicated—only slightly, though. In order to understand the process, it is imperative to think of images not at the continuous-tone photograph you are used to but rather as a series of colored dots. If you closely examine a color photograph that appears in a newspaper, you will notice that the image is not made of continuous color but of a series of colored dots that blend together to create a continuous color. When viewed from a distance, these tiny dots, if small enough and grouped closely enough together, give the eye the impression of a continuous-tone photograph. A similar solution has been developed for the computer.

To understand how this works, we need to understand computer color systems. In the computer three primary colors exist, red, green, and blue. All other colors can be created using just these three colors. White and black, of course, are, respectively, the presence or absence of all colors.

If we decide that there are 255 different levels of saturation (amounts of color) for each color, we can represent a roughly 16 million possible different colors using the three components red green blue (R, G, B). For example, true primary red would be represented by R = 255, G = 0, and B = 0, since green and blue have no input in true primary red. Every other color could then be "mixed" using different levels of the three primaries. Although there are differences between various color systems that change the mixtures of the numbers, these differences are not important to our discussion. To help further illustrate this concept, think of your local hardware store paint section. If you ask for a custom-mixed color, the technician, using a reference chart, will add certain amounts of each primary tint to a white base, to reach the desired color. The RGB color system in the computer is essentially no different.

Once we have translated each color into its individual components, those colors' numbers are stored as their binary equivalents. In the example of primary red (255, 0, 0), they would be (11111111, 00000000, 00000000).

The computer's graphic processing card can replicate any color simply by setting the value of the individual pixels of light on the monitor to that combination of values. Pixels, also known as picture elements, are the tiny little dots of color you see when you look very closely at your monitor. Depending on the file format of the graphic image, these values are stored more or less sequentially and then pasted on the monitor screen, resulting in millions of tiny colored dots that fool the eye in to seeing a coherent shape. When dealing with how information is stored by a computer, no discussion would be complete without addressing the ever-popular music file. Regardless of the format used, whether Ogg-Vorbis, MP3, Mpeg-4, or some other proprietary format, all music files have one thing in common. At some point a conversion of the analog music signal into its digital equivalent was done (this discussion overlooks digitally created synthetic music). Earlier I mentioned the differences between digital and analog signals. As I explained, the analog quality of our trumpet note gives it a frequency, which is measured in hertz. Hertz is nothing more than a measurement of cycles per second where 1 hertz equals 1 cycle per second. If the trumpet is sounding the note commonly known as A above middle C, its frequency is roughly 440 hertz (Hz).[2] This means that our wave will cycle just over 440 times per second. This simplified explanation of hertz is important because it helps to understand the simplified explanation of analog to digital conversion.

In analog-to-digital conversion, often abbreviated ADC or A/D, the sound wave is measured at many points in time. These measurements, known as samples, are then converted into binary numbers. The number of measurements of the analog sound wave determines how accurately the sound is reproduced.[3] Common sampling rates are 44.1 kilohertz (kHz) for CD audio or 48 kHz for DVD audio. The process works this way: The waveform of the piece of music—in our example the trumpet playing the note A above middle C—is measured 44,100 times per second. Because a musical note is essentially a sine wave, the values of that wave at 44,100 places along its curve are measured and converted into their digital equivalent. The resulting binary numbers become the digital audio wave file.[4]

When playing back the file, the digital data is converted back into an analog signal, which drives an output device like speakers no differently than if the conversion had never taken place.

If this example of digital storage of an audio file has completely confused you, relax. Understanding the complexities of ADC is not a requirement of understanding computer forensics. What is important is that you grasp the concept of how analog, or nondigital, data, whether it is music, video, photos, or documents, is converted into binary information, which is the only thing computers understand.

Now we can look at what the computer system does with that information once it has it. Computers are inanimate objects. They can do only what we as humans tell them to. Therefore, we must discuss how we tell them what to do.

Computer programs are the fundamental way in which we tell computers what to do. These programs range in function from entire operating systems, such as Windows XP or Linux, to simple calculator applications. Regardless of complexity, they all tell the computer what to do using a predefined set of instructions known as code.

In the beginning, computers had their instructions hardwired into them. As technology progressed, and devices such as magnetic memory emerged, later computers had their programs coded, in machine language, into their memory. Eventually, computers developed to the point where their system memory was both flexible and substantial. With these advances the user's ability to program the computer on the fly increased. Coincidentally with these advances in technology came advances in programming.[5]

Computer scientists originally were restricted to coding instructions into the computer in only binary numbers, which was cumbersome and highly error prone; by the mid-1950s, however, they had developed high-level programming languages. As mentioned earlier, FORTRAN, the first of these languages, allowed programmers to tell the computer what to do easily. Although unreadable directly by the computer itself, translators and compilers convert this high-level language into machine-readable code, which is executed by the computer.

Today there are many more high-level programming languages than in 1954, but they all do roughly the same thing that FORTRAN did when it was released to the public in 1959. FORTRAN is still currently in wide use, which speaks volumes about its functionality.

The difference between computer programs and operating systems is a fine one, but one that is extremely important to forensic examiners. A computer operating system (OS) is, in actuality, nothing more than a more robust computer program. The difference is it that the OS, unlike a computer program, loads into memory immediately after the computer boots up and takes over control of the entire computer system. This "minor" difference has both benefits and drawbacks, depending on which side of the fence you are on.

The benefits include relieving users from more mundane input/output functions, such as telling the computer how to print a document, where to store a file, or how to display a graphic on the screen. The drawbacks include insulating users from some of the more powerful functions of the computer, slowing the computer's operation, and ultimately taking control of the computer away from users.

Whether they like operating systems or not, examiners must deal with them. As stated, the OS loads into system memory immediately once the computer boots up and takes over control of the system. Once the OS takes control, background processes, such as disk access, code and process loading and maintenance operations take place. To average users, these processes are both transparent and a welcome part of the OS. To computer examiners, however, they can spell the end of the case. For reasons that will be explained in later chapters, these uncontrolled disk accesses and program loads change the value of entries in key system files and overwrite potential evidence in areas known as slack space. In addition, on boot up, the integrity of the once-valuable evidence will be compromised and may become worthless in court. Understanding this fundamental aspect of the OS is the key to ensuring that any evidence seized is usable in court.

OUTPUT

Output is about getting the information, after processing, back out of the computer and into the user's hands. As stated earlier, output takes many forms, but one common form is printed material. For computer examiners, printed output often contains some of the most powerful and nonvolatile evidence in a case.

As cautioned earlier, when you are considering the different components of a computer system, do not limit yourself to traditional notions of what constitute computers. Do not overlook the fact that most modern printers have a substantial amount of RAM memory, and many even have their own processing unit to help speed up the printing process. Although not a computer by most definitions, these mini-processing units might contain valuable evidentiary data.

Also included in the output category are monitors, those ever-flattening video screens that serve multiple purposes, from surrogate television screens, to simple scratch pads. With the exception of their efficiency, which has translated into size reduction, computer monitors have changed very little over the years and continue to perform the same basic functions they always have: They allow users to watch real-time output while interacting with the computer. Unlike the printer output system, monitors operate in real time and display data only momentarily. This fleeting glimpse into the heart of the computer can provide valuable information.

CONCLUSION

In this chapter, I have tried to provide enough information for readers to understand how computers operate and the major components that comprise most systems and have offered some insight into the pitfalls that computer forensic technicians face. Armed with a fundamental understanding of how computers operate, you should be better able to digest explanations in later chapters.

In coming chapters, I will help you build on the knowledge you have developed in this chapter and gain a better understanding of the forensic examination process and the limitations of the field.

NOTES

1. *The Columbia Electronic Encyclopedia,* 6th ed., on Infoplease, s.v. "ASCII," www.infoplease.com/ce6/sci/A0804949.html.
2. Dave Benson, *Music: A Mathematical Offering* (London: Cambridge University Press, 2006). Also available at www.maths.abdn.ac.uk/~bensondj/html/music.pdf, pp. 17–19.
3. Ken C. Pohlmann, *Principles of Digital Audio,* 5th ed. (New York: McGraw-Hill, 2005), pp. 63, 65, 418, 646.
4. Ibid.
5. See generally Paul E. Cerruzzi, *The History of Modern Computing,* 2nd ed. (Cambridge, MA: MIT Press, 2003).

SUGGESTED READING

Ballora, Mark. *Essentials of Music Technology.* Upper Saddle River, NJ: Prentice-Hall, 2003.

Cohen, Daniel I. A. *Introduction to Computer Theory,* 2nd ed. New York: John Wiley & Sons, 1991.

Ifeachor, Emmanuel, and Barrie Jervis. *Digital Signal Processing: A Practical Approach,* 2nd ed. Upper Saddle River, NJ: Prentice-Hall, 2001.

Lyons, Richard G. *Understanding Digital Signal Processing,* 2nd ed. Upper Saddle River, NJ: Prentice-Hall, 2004.

Maran, Ruth. *Computers Simplified,* 5th ed. Foster City, CA: IDG Books Worldwide, 2000.

Norton, Peter. *Peter Norton's Computer Fundamentals,* 4th ed. New York: McGraw-Hill, 2000.

3

PRESERVATION AND COLLECTION OF DIGITAL EVIDENCE

INTRODUCTION

Chapter 2 provided a basic understanding of computers and how they operate. With this knowledge in place, we can turn our attention to the nuts and bolts of what computer forensic technicians do: seize and analyze evidence. Whether we are discussing seizure and analysis of computers in terms of a criminal investigation or the civil discovery process, the process proceeds according to a fairly uniform blueprint. This blueprint usually has five stages: preservation, collection, analysis, re-creation, and rendering of the opinion. In this chapter, I discuss the preservation and collection phases of the process, what they involve, and some of the common pitfalls that confront investigators. I will discuss analysis, recreation and rendering of an expert opinion in later chapters.

RULES OF EVIDENCE

When dealing with evidence, the underlying principle that guides us is admissibility. The admissibility concept in turn drives our efforts to preserve the evidence, since admissibility dictates whether evidence ultimately will be allowed into court to advance the case. Even though this is not a book on evidence, because digital evidence differs from more traditional forms of evidence in a couple significant ways, a few words about admissibility and digital evidence are in order.

One of the underlying tenets to admissibility of evidence is the notion of reliability. In our system, we hope to ensure, as best we can, that only those who are guilty, or liable if it is a civil case, are held responsible. To best serve this goal, certain rules and procedures have been instituted; chief among them are our notions of evidentiary reliability.

Regardless of which rule we examine, we will find that ultimately it is designed to help ensure that cases are prosecuted with only the most reliable evidence. For example, a common example is the best evidence rule, which holds, in part, that only originals of documents (with some exceptions) are admissible in court.

In this day and age, the best evidence rule might seem somewhat antiquated; however, the basic rationale for its existence is still valid. It is in place because we believe that originals are a more reliable representation of the actual document and, as such, we should use them whenever possible. This rule requiring originals ensures reliability and thus helps us feel more secure in the outcomes of our legal proceedings.

In the realm of digital evidence, the notion of reliability takes on an entirely new significance, and often it is one that can be inadvertently overlooked. When nondigital evidence is seized, ensuring the integrity and reliability of that evidence is usually pretty straightforward. It is often packaged, sealed, and transported in a way that we can reconstruct the chain of custody perfectly. With digital evidence, securing evidence may become more difficult in ways that untrained observers might not immediately recognize. For this reason, preservation of evidence is often the most crucial moment in a case involving digital evidence.

Computers do a large number of things behind the scenes. At no point is it more important to understand this fact than when undertaking the actual preservation of digital evidence. As the preservation stage is the key step in the digital evidence recovery process, everything that happens at this stage will influence the outcome. If an investigator blunders here, the evidence is lost forever and no amount of tweaking will bring it back.

PRESERVATION

The seizure process begins with preserving the evidence. Whether in the digital world or the more traditional world, preservation ensures that the evidence has not been changed from the field to the point in time when it is presented in court. Without this crucial stage, much of your evidence will be lost to suppression.

In the digital world, preservation means something a little different from what it means in the nondigital world. For example, consider the case of a forged check. An investigator responding to the scene would most likely take possession of the check, place it in an envelope, mark it, seal it, and take custody of it by having the person from whom it was seized sign the check over on an evidence receipt. Then the investigator would transport the evidence to the station for storage in a secure evidence facility, where the custodian would sign for it and place it into storage until it is needed.

This procedure happens hundreds of times a day in police departments all across the United States. With no further action on the part of the investigator, the check will most likely pass the test of admissibility. By packaging, sealing, and documenting who has had possession of this item, the investigator will be able to testify that no alterations have been made and that the item being introduced in court is the very same item, taken from the victim.

In the digital world, although the same basic procedure applies, the nature of the evidence makes preservation much trickier. One reason for this added level of difficulty is the fact that digital evidence is not always apparent. Going back to the check example, the check is always apparent; we can see it, recognize it, touch it, and manipulate it. Conversely, digital evidence is apparent only when the computer is turned on. If I seize a laptop computer, the laptop itself, while possibly evidence in its own right, is of real value only when I can get to what is inside. Unlike a book, whose pages I can peruse by simply opening it, a computer must be turned on. The very process of turning on the computer will in fact change the evidence. These changes, which are done in the background by the operating system (OS), can destroy the reliability of evidence. The process of starting a computer is the functional equivalent of opening a book, erasing several lines of the text, and replacing that text with something new—every time you open it.

Likewise, the same issues arise when turning off digital evidence. When turning off a computer, the OS, in all its efficiency, takes care of hundreds of routine housekeeping tasks, such as closing open files, flushing buffers, and shifting things around so that the next time you hit the "on" switch, everything runs in a trouble-free way. Again, these processes, controlled by the OS and entirely beyond user control, happen in the background. With the exception of a few clicks of the hard drive and flashes of some light-emitting diodes (LEDs), they are completely transparent to the user. Like the start-up process, this process is the functional equivalent of erasing several lines from the pages of a book and replacing them with new text every time you close your book. These changes are serious when considered in the context of the requirement of evidence preservation.

To make matters even more complicated, these processes happen not only when the computer (or any digital evidence for that matter) is powered up and down, but also when other things happen. For example, as seemingly harmless as a simple movement of the mouse might first appear, it can in fact cause irreparable damage to evidence. Although often it is not fatal, the action of moving the mouse causes the computer actually to shift information around in memory in order for the OS to respond to the user's request and reposition the cursor to its new location.

Will the simple act of moving a mouse ruin a case? Probably not, since it is unlikely that moving the mouse will cause changes in the files on the hard drive (which is where the majority of evidence will be). However, it will change the data that is stored in random access memory (RAM), which can include things such as passwords, file information, and system state data. All of these things, depending on the type of case, can be very important.

For these reasons, one of the most important rules to reinforce to inexperienced investigators is that doing anything, and I do mean *anything,* to a computer runs the risk of changing evidence. And as with nondigital evidence, every change that is made to evidence must be both documented and explained in court.

Now that I have driven home the importance of keeping evidence in its most pristine state as possible, I can loosen up somewhat. From the earlier text, it might appear that no alterations to evidence can ever be made during an investigation. Although I have been preaching about the need to preserve and maintain the integrity of the evidence, this rule is neither inflexible nor unreasonable. As an illustration of this, I will rely on a real-world, nondigital example.

In a narcotics case where drugs are seized, one of the elements that the prosecutor must prove is that the substance seized was in fact a controlled narcotic, let us say heroin. In order to prove that the substance is heroin, the police lab must run some tests and a qualified expert must testify to the results—something that Americans see dramatized every week on television police dramas. However, the act of testing the substance is usually a destructive process. The chemist must use a small amount of the substance, which is consumed during the test, to verify its chemical compound. The consumption of this sample, regardless of how minute, changes the evidence. The chemist who began with 1 gram of heroin might end with .999 grams of heroin. This reduction of 1/1000th of a gram of the heroin, while extremely small, is in fact a change in the evidence. Based on the requirement of preservation, this process would seem to render the evidence inadmissible.

Although changes in evidence may render it inadmissible, certain exceptions to this rule apply—the previous analysis is one such example. The rules of evidence are not so inflexible as to make the administration of justice impossible. Destructive testing is acceptable in this and similar cases, and because such tests are required as part of the investigative process, they will not result in evidentiary exclusion.

In the world of digital evidence, this principle also applies. Even though the admonitions discussed previously are still true, you need to keep in mind two things. First, it is highly unlikely, if not entirely impossible for an investigator to seize digital evidence without changing something. Second, that although the general rules on the admissibility of evidence exclude evidence that has been altered, some alteration will be acceptable as long as it is both necessary and well documented.

Given this fact, the way in which investigators approach the scene of a case involving digital evidence is very important. Strict observation of the rule to "change nothing"—similar to the Hippocratic Oath, which states "first do no harm"—followed by impeccable record keeping during a seizure can start investigators on a solid path toward a successful seizure and admissible evidence.

In the preservation stage, investigators will have to make some very difficult decisions: whether to turn on, turn off, or disassemble or reassemble a computer system. Investigators also may confront a choice of whether to conduct a "live" analysis of the system in situ or to transport the device to a lab for later examination. All of these decisions will be dictated by the individual circumstances of each case and will influence what occurs during the next stage. While no hard and fast rules are available for every situation, the cautions about changing nothing and documenting everything are valuable tools to guide investigators.

The decisions about whether computers should be turned off, turned on, shut down using the OS, or simply unplugged should be made by a trained professional after carefully evaluating all the possible ramifications given the needs of the case. Here my aim it to provide a better understanding of the options computer forensic technicians confront on each case.

In some cases, the capture of volatile data, such as system settings, log-on information, or RAM slack—more on RAM slack later—might be the most important part of the case. If so, turning off the computer will be the wrong path to take. Conversely, if investigators believe that all the evidence they will need is contained on the hard drive, a computer shutdown would probably be the appropriate course of action. And if that course of action is chosen, more options exist—orderly shutdown or simply pulling the plug—each with its own unique advantages and drawbacks. Either way, some information will be compromised. It is up to the investigators, relying on their skill, training, and experience, to decide which the most reasonable choice is. To reiterate, no particular course of action may be more or less correct than another, and each choice will have both advantages and disadvantages; however, proper documentation by the investigator and reliance on sound investigative practice will be the key to deciding whether the evidence ultimately will see the inside of the court room.

In summary, all actions you take in regard to digital evidence—turning it on, turning it off, or simply moving the mouse—will change data within the device. These changes, while unavoidable, have the power to render digital evidence inadmissible. Because in many cases the digital evidence may be the only evidence, such changes this can be the death knell for your legal action. To avoid this unpleasant outcome, investigators must use extreme caution when doing anything to a digital device and must document any actions they do take. Only by doing these things with every case can investigators have even the remotest hope of preserving the evidence.

COLLECTION

Once the digital evidence has been preserved, whether by seizing the entire device for transport or simply taking physical custody of it, the next stage of the process can begin. In this stage unavoidable alterations will occur; as already explained, investigators must carefully document their actions. This stage is the point of no return.

If the evidence is properly preserved, it can remain in that state, unaltered, for a relatively long period of time. A computer that has been seized in a power-off state can theoretically remain unchanged for a very long period of time. Until you turn it on, it will remain in the exact same condition. Unfortunately, in this condition the evidence is of no value to us. Just like my example of the book, we do not know what is inside until we open it to read the pages. Turning on our computer allows us to "read the pages."

When we cross the point of no return, we will be changing things, albeit with a purpose, and once those things have been changed, we can never undo them. Therefore, it is during this stage that investigators must take the most care. Thorough documentation and careful planning are essential; otherwise everything that follows will be meaningless.

In most cases, the collection of evidence from a digital device will progress in a predictable pattern. Regardless of the type of device, brand, or configuration, investigators should take specific steps to ensure that as little data as possible is changed. These steps are flexible but are applicable to nearly all cases with only minor changes and adaptations.

As I have mentioned several times, all operating systems change computer data behind the scenes. It is the job of investigators either to reduce the impact of this or to eliminate it altogether. In order to do this, there are a few options available. Again, depending on the dictates of each case, one choice might be more or less appropriate. In a case where the device is seized in a power-off state, the only place evidence can be found is in the permanent storage device (as I have explained, "permanent" is a relative term). For most digital devices, this will be the hard drive; however, peripheral devices such as flash or thumb drives might contain the evidence. The point is that the system's temporary storage devices, the on-board RAM (that part of a computer where instructions code and processing data is stored) will not contain any data before the computer is powered up. At this point investigators generally confront a dilemma: Power up the system to access the data or remove the storage device and collect the data on a secure workstation in the computer lab.

Removal of the disk might be the more appropriate alternative in cases where the integrity of the suspect system is in question or where questions exist about whether connecting to peripheral interfaces like disk drives and storages devices might pose problems. These issues might center on compatibility between the collection devices used by investigators and the suspect computer system. Perhaps the suspect system has too few or incompatible connection options, which prohibit investigators from temporarily installing an evidence hard drive onto which they can copy the suspect drive. If so, investigators avoid the need to boot the system by taking the system back to the laboratory.

On-site capture of the evidence might be more appropriate in circumstances where immediacy is important. In some cases, search warrants authorizing the collection of digital evidence might require investigators to conduct an on-site collection because the suspect's computer system is a high-sensitivity system, and removal of the disk will present unwarranted inconvenience for the suspect. Remember, in criminal cases, suspects are always presumed innocent;

judges, ever mindful of this fact, try to balance the needs of investigators to collect potential evidence against the rights of the suspect or defendant.

If on-site capture is chosen, investigators must now ensure that as little data is changed as possible. In cases where the system is turned off, the most important goal is to prevent alteration of the hard drive. This is where our discussion of computers in Chapter 2 should prove valuable. We must understand the start-up process of a computer to grasp what happens from an investigative standpoint.

As you will recall, a computer is entirely worthless without instructions. These instructions come from programmers. Programmers tell the computer what to do through program code, which, if written in a high-level language such as C or C++, is translated by the compiler into machine-readable 0s and 1s. When the "on" button is pressed, a computer must obtain its instructions from somewhere. In most cases the first place these instructions come from are the system BIOS.

BIOS (defined as basic input output system or basic integrated operating system) is responsible for offering basic functionality at start-up. This small self-contained program code, part of the system hardware, is usually only a few kilobytes in size. It allows the computer to go through its power-on self-test (POST) routine, which diagnoses its health status, then loads the very basic driver data to allow access to onboard systems, such as drives, displays, and whatever hardware devices are installed. These stubs of code are what ultimately control most of the computer's functionality and are the doorways through which the higher-level software gains access to the computer's hardware.

Once the BIOS is loaded and the system has confirmed that it is healthy, the computer must receive further instructions. In theory, this information could be part of the BIOS, but in reality, the OS usually provides the next set of instructions. Once the BIOS completes the necessary housekeeping required to ensure functionality, it instructs the computer to load an external OS. The BIOS could not care less what form the OS takes. It is just as happy to find a version of Windows as it is Linux. All the BIOS does is tell the computer where to start to look for the OS. In most default configurations, the computer first looks for a floppy drive, next for a CD drive, then finally for a hard disk, which the system accesses based on the physical disks installed, not the logical disks.[1] In some configurations, the BIOS can even search a network for the OS. The order in which the system searches for an OS is very important. It is at this boot-up stage that investigators must intervene.

Immediately at start-up, investigators must access the BIOS setup screen. On most systems, this screen can be accessed by pressing a key designated by the particular BIOS manufacturer as the BIOS Setup access key. On many systems this is the Del key. Access to the BIOS setup program allows investigators to choose the order in which the system looks for the OS. In most systems, investigators want to select the floppy drive; now that many computers are being manufactured without floppy drives, then the next most likely choice for investigators is the CD/DVD ROM drive. The most important thing is to select a device *other* than the hard drive.

By changing the location in which the BIOS searches for the OS, investigators are creating the opportunity to circumvent the natural start-up process. Once the BIOS information has been either changed or verified, investigators restart the system after inserting a special disk into whichever drive they have selected as the start-up drive. This special disk contains a very bare-bones configuration of software that will allow the computer to complete the start-up process, without loading a full version of the OS. What it loads instead, in most cases, is a special disk-write blocking program which prevents all destructive access to the hard drive, and a small selection of essential programs.

The procedure just outlined can vary. For example, in some circumstances, investigators may use a device known as a hardware write blocker, which consists of computer components that are installed between the computer's motherboard, which is the circuit board all the components connect to, and its hard drive. They are usually fairly simple to connect, and they physically prevent the motherboard from writing anything onto the hard drive. Although it is ideal to install such a device, operational requirements such as hardware incompatibility, may occasionally prohibit doing so. In this case, investigators must rely on the software write blocker, which does the functional equivalent, only through a software-based method.

The installation of these small kernels of software programs allows investigators just enough functionality to collect the evidence data. Remember, at this point investigators have no interest in analyzing the evidence, merely collecting it in a safe and defensible manner. Analysis will come later.

Once the system has been booted up, write blocking has been enabled through either a hardware or a software solution, and investigators have gained control of the system, they must collect the evidence, using tools known as imagers.

Disk imaging software allows investigators to make exact duplicates of the suspect's hard drive. This is more complicated than it sounds because there are essentially two ways in which computer data can be copied by the OS. The first, and most common, does not make an exact copy but only copies important information, such as visible files and program data. This is the type of copy that usually occurs when you drag and drop a file from a folder on your hard drive onto your floppy drive or create a CD from a group of files on your hard drive. Even if you make a complete backup copy of a hard drive, the normal copy process leaves behind an array of information that is highly valuable to investigators.

A wide variety of imagers is commercially available and, as you might expect, each has its limitations; however, most offer what investigators require—a bit-for-bit, exact duplicate of the hard drive. As discussed in Chapter 1, every piece of information, whether document, program, music file, or photograph, is stored by a computer as nothing more than 0s and 1s. Computers have been designed to operate most efficiently; as a result, there have been some compromises reached during their evolution. One such compromise involves disk architecture. Each disk is formatted in order to optimize both storage space and access speed. To do this, the entire disk is divided into small chunks of real estate, and each chunk is viewed by the OS as a unit. When the OS needs to write a piece of information to the disk, it places it in a chunk. The entire chunk is allocated, regardless of whether the information can fill it in its entirety or not.

To make this more clear, think of a one-gallon plastic jug and a cup of water. Our gallon jug is fixed; it cannot expand or contract. If we pour the cup of water into the jug, although it only fills a small portion of it, the jug's volume remains the same. Likewise, if we want to maintain the integrity of the water, we cannot add anything else to that storage container. It is marked as being in use by the water. The hard drive is no different. Even though this method of allocating storage space is pretty efficient, it can pose problems for investigators. One such problem arises because of something known as file slack, or drive slack.

File slack exists because the computer tries to be most efficient when reusing storage space and because the way in which computers erase data is not consistent with the normal definition of erasure. When a computer erases data, it does not really erase it. Instead, it makes an electronic mark in the file that makes it appear to the OS that the file is gone. The file actually still exists on the hard drive, but the OS no longer recognizes it. Then, when searching for empty disk space to place new files, the computer can write the new file over the space where the old file, which still exists, was stored. When this happens, if the new file has fewer bytes than the old file, the end pieces of the old file continue to remain in the tail end of the storage space. It still appears invisible to the OS, but actually exists in the form of 0s and 1s on the disk. The hard disk space from the end of the new file to the end of the actual storage unit (to top rim of our one-gallon jug) is known as file slack. As you can see, it is possible that old file information may remain in this slack area—information that could be of great value to an investigator.

Traditional copying leaves the file slack behind and copies only the actual file entries. Disk imagers make a bit-for-bit copy: an exact image of the old disk, file slack and all. This bit-for-bit image is very important because it allows investigators to get an exact duplicate of the original. It is this copy—or actually a copy of the copy—that investigators will use for analysis.

Depending on individual functionality, imaging software can provide an array of options, such as copying the hard drive to a DVD, CD, or another hard drive of different dimensions. In early versions of most imaging software, the geometry of target disks had to be identical to that of the suspect disks. (Geometry is the actual internal layout of the disk that defines how data is stored. It includes things such as the number of sectors, cylinders, and heads available.) Most commercial imaging software available today have overcome these limitations.

Once the imaging process is complete, investigators will, in most cases, securely store the original seized hard drive, ensuring that it is safe from erasure hazards, such as electrical current, magnetic influence, and tampering. Once this has been done, the most complicated portions of the process have been completed. While the analysis and reconstruction process requires great knowledge of computers, various operating systems, and an almost endless array of programs, the point in the investigation when the most evidentiary damage can be done is past. The suspect's hard drive is securely tucked away in evidence storage, and everything from here will be completed on a backup copy of the imaged drive. Therefore, even if investigators make a mistake, the worst-case scenario requires nothing more than making a second copy of the image. The evidence hard drive is never again touched. In other words, most fatal mistakes that can be made will be made in the steps up to this point.

That doesn't mean that the analysis stage and reconstruction stages are easier. In fact, they are more complicated. The reality of forensic examination is that given a solid foundation in computers, a standard list of procedures to follow, and proper software and hardware, the average investigator can perform most evidentiary seizures. Examination and interpretation of computer operating systems—all computer operating systems, especially the more arcane ones, however, require a very strong knowledge of all aspects of computers. Add to that the fact that the results of the analysis must be explained in a way that others can duplicate the findings, and it is clear that the most demanding portion of the job lies ahead.

Even though I have characterized the seizure portion of the process as being relatively straightforward, a number of twists and turns can influence the complexity of the job. Often investigators can plan around these twists and turns. For example, incompatibility of hardware and software can complicate the seizure process. Most of the time, however, these operational concerns are discovered before the actual seizure is begun. Likewise, with the nearly exponential growth of storage space in the past few years, seizing larger and larger hard drives, even those approaching the terabyte (TB) level (a TB equals 1,000 gigabytes), is a real possibility. In fact, in some network or enterprise environments, storage arrays can easily approach 15 or more terabytes.

And on the subject of storage arrays, most new computers have built-in RAID capabilities. RAID stands for either redundant array of independent disks, or redundant array of inexpensive disks, depending on which source you consult. Either way, the end result is a storage system that is composed of several individual hard drives, chained together through one device, usually a hardware controller, that act like one single device. RAIDs can be set up in several combinations, depending on what the goal is. Computer forensic investigators often encounter two configurations. The first configuration is for data security. In this configuration, every disk acts as a backup for the others and information that is written to one disk is also written to the backup. In that way, if the original disk fails, the backup is available. RAIDs also can be structured to increase storage size and access speed. In this configuration, all the disks are made to appear as one big hard drive, but each is written to individually. Therefore, if I have two 100 GB disks arrayed together in this configuration, it appears that I have one single 200 GB disk. In some circumstances, because I am writing different sequential information to both disks simultaneously, it is possible to have a portion of a file on disk A and another portion of the same file on disk B.

With most modern software imaging programs, arrays present no problem. Aside from possible storage problems associated with imaging a 20 terabyte array, modern imaging programs can handle both hardware- and software-based array systems. However, investigators must be cognizant of their existence so that they can plan around their own limitations.

CONCLUSION

This chapter should have made obvious that the groundwork I laid in earlier chapters was not wasted ink. Instead, it began what we have picked up in this chapter. The physical process of seizing a computer may be basically straightforward, but it is imperative that you understand both the hardware and the software issues.

As we move forward into the next chapter, I will pick up this thread and begin to explore the analysis process that computer forensic technicians go through when handling an average case. As always, results may vary, and each individual case will often dictate the particular methods or order of steps the investigator will use.

NOTE

1. Physical disks are the actual number of hard drives installed on the computer. Logical disks are created by the computer's operating system but do not directly correspond to the number of physical hard drives on the computer. For example, a computer may have one physical hard drive, which the system assigns drive letter "C." In addition, the system may create several partitions on that drive and designate them as drives "G," "H," and "I." These logical disks, although not individual physical hard drives, are capable of storing information just as though they were

SUGGESTED READING

Brown, Christopher L. T. *Computer Evidence: Collection & Preservation*. Hingham, MA: Charles River Media, 2006.

Nelson, Bill, Amelia Phillips, Frank Enfinger, and Christopher Steuart. *Guide to Computer Forensics and Investigations*, 2nd ed. Boston: Thomson-Course Technology, 2006.

Vacca, John R. *Computer Forensics: Computer Crime Scene Investigation*. Hingham, MA: Charles River Media, 2002.

4

ANALYSIS OF DIGITAL EVIDENCE

INTRODUCTION

With the highly sensitive task of digital evidence collection out of the way, computer investigators can now settle in for a careful and detailed analysis of the data collected. In Chapter 3, you learned that the tasks associated with the preservation and collection of evidence are riddled with opportunities to compromise the evidence. One false move, and the information contained in the computer's memory or on the hard drive is irrevocably altered. This alteration, you also learned, may be grounds for exclusion of any evidence that is left behind.

However, by carefully following industry-accepted practices and using appropriate tools, such as write blockers and hard drive imagers, investigators can greatly reduce the amount of data that is altered in a system. The investigators' next task is no easier, but the risk of evidentiary damage is much less—provided they follow the proper procedures.

In this chapter, we embark on the portion of the investigators' task that usually takes the greatest amount of time—the analysis and recreation of the evidence. Depending on the nature of the investigation, the size of the disk, and how much background information is available, the task may take hundreds of hours—or it may take a few as three or four. When searching a suspect's hard drive, investigators will rely on a combination of very powerful tools and good old-fashioned hard work to comb through every crevice of a drive looking for tiny fragments of information that might just serve as the final nail in the suspect's coffin.

FORENSIC ANALYSIS

It is impossible to dictate which method of analysis to use in different cases. The specifics of a case often prescribe the order in which investigators should proceed. Depending on what investigators are looking for, different approaches and search orders are more practical than others. Instead of recommending one particular order in which investigators should proceed, instead I offer insight into where potential evidence might be found and leave it to the trained professional to determine the exact search order.

Before I discuss the basics of searching a computer for evidence, I am going to digress slightly and discuss some of the tools available to computer investigators. There is no "silver bullet" in this field, and often investigators will use more than one tool on the same case. These tools can be divided into two groups: stand-alone tools and application suites.

A stand-alone tool is a discrete computer program that performs one particular function in the analysis process. For example, the computer program WinHex, by X-Ways Software (www.x-ways.net/winhex/), is one in a group of utilities that has become very popular among forensic experts. Although WinHex was not originally directed at the forensic market, its power, albeit in a limited area, is great, and it has developed a fairly strong following over the years.

Using WinHex, investigators can quickly and easily begin a bit-by-bit examination of a hard drive, viewing the data on the disk in both hexadecimal and ASCII (American Standard Code for Information Exchange) notation. As you will recall from Chapter 2, hexadecimal numbers are an alternative notation form that computer experts use as shorthand notation for binary numbers. This powerful tool makes searching for individual groupings of characters or words much easier.

Another stand-alone tool is distributed by Paraben Software under the name Email Examiner (www.paraben-forensics.com); it offers exactly the functionality its name suggests. While other e-mail examination programs are incorporated into the larger, more all-in-one suites I discuss next, stand-alone applications often provide a more direct or more versatile solution.

There are several very powerful and very popular application suites on the market. All are equally well regarded and robust, and all come with a pretty hefty price tag attached. Of these, two probably receive more press than the others: Encase by Guidance Software (www.guidancesoftware.com/) and AccessData FTK (Forensic Toolkit) (www.accessdata.com/products/). Both these tools can run under a Windows OS and can examine data across platforms. Because they are suites, they have integrated functionality across the forensic examination process and offer a one-stop-shopping approach that gives forensic technicians the ability to seize, collect, and analyze digital evidence all under one platform. As with all software, each program has some disadvantages, and often investigators will use many different tools. One of the great benefits of these suites is the built-in logging and report generation function.

As I have stressed, thorough documentation is absolutely essential to defensible computer examination. Suites such as Encase and FTK gather every move investigators make and all the file information they collect. The suites then collate this information and format into a convenient report that investigators can use for further investigation or courtroom presentations. As you will see shortly, keeping track of things like file access date and time stamps and directory structures on large computer systems can be difficult without the assistance of one of these suites.

The bottom line, however, is that even investigators who utilize one of these major software suites often use different stand-alone programs, such as disk imagers and password cracking software, as well, depending on the needs of each case.

Analysis suites are extremely powerful tools, and like all powerful computer programs, they have fairly steep learning curves. Although they can do everything investigators could need, it is up to investigators to master them in order to take full advantage of their potential. Just like a painter, given a brush and the three primary colors, has the tools to paint images as beautiful as those in the Sistine Chapel, it is doubtful that he will, unless he also possesses the skill of Michelangelo.

Before beginning any search, investigators must have a strong understanding of the type of case before them. For example, a child pornography case will have a completely different search pattern from a corporate espionage case. Although both might involve image files and documents, particular keywords are more likely to produce matches than others in each case, and as you will learn, key word searches are some of the most powerful tools in your toolkit.

When investigators begin a case, they usually have a flexible yet preconceived idea about where to search and what to search for. This plan of attack is based on their knowledge of the facts of the case and the skill level of the suspect. Not all cases will have the same level of challenge associated with them and will not require the same depth of analysis. For example, novice computer users are much less likely to have created hidden partitions on their hard drive in which they could hide evidence than would highly skilled computer hackers. While hiding a drive partition is easily within the skills of average users, it can be a bit tricky, and novice users are unlikely to go to the effort to conceal their activities to that degree.

Nevertheless, all computer investigators are trained to consider all possibilities and will examine the partition information at least cursorily to make sure the numbers all match the system information.

Now that you understand that each investigation will proceed on its own schedule and particular path unique to its facts, we can discuss some of the general things that computer investigators can expect to find and things that they will do during a forensic examination. First and foremost, investigators must examine the drive for any visible evidence. Suspicious executable program files are of great importance, either because they are out of place or because they are known to corroborate the suspected offense.

Tools that help hide evidence, encrypt data, and destroy files are all legal; however, if they are on a suspect's computer, investigators may consider a different course of action in searching the system or might consider alternative plans of action.

Other items of interest are files with suspicious-sounding names or names that investigators would expect to find based on the suspect's crime. For example, graphic files with suggestive names on a computer of a kiddie-porn suspect are all great clues that can help direct a search.

Access information is of paramount importance. Every file that is created by a computer should be assigned a date and time stamp. This stamp is updated every time someone opens or accesses the file. Prior to examining the file, it is important for investigators to record and make note of the last access date and time. Otherwise, it may be impossible to establish that the file was opened last on a particular date, say the date the suspect was last known to be in the country. Analysis tools can assist in this process by automatically recording all this critical system data and making a record of all system and file access dates.

If for some reason investigators fail to record this information, all may not be lost yet. Because they were following proper protocol and examining a copy of the copied hard drive,[1] the information still exists on the original copy. Therefore, this newly made copy of the data drive will reveal the accurate numbers.

On most occasions, one of the first things on the list of things to do will be to examine the disk for file slack. As I explained earlier, due to the way in which computer operating systems allocate storage space, small unusable portions of disk space are scattered around the user's disk. Although these spaces do not contain actual files that the system can read, they may contain other information: fragments of old, partially deleted files and random access memory (RAM) slack which is just like file slack except it occurs in the random access memory of the computer.

When a computer saves a file to disk, the information, say a word processing document, has a size in bytes and an ending point. This file size directly relates to how much storage space is required for the file—not just on the disk, but also in system memory. When the computer system's memory is flushed to store the file on disk, such as when you close your word processing program, instead of calculating the exact location of the end of the file in system memory and saving only that portion, the system instead saves the entire block to the drive. Because the computer's system memory is constantly in use, shifting information in, out, and around its storage locations, the chances of these "extra" memory locations being completely empty are very slim. Instead, "leftover" data is there, and will be flushed to the drive along with the word processing file.

The example in Exhibit 4.1 should help.

In Exhibit 4.1, each cell represents a single byte of system memory storage. Taken together, they comprise a block of memory that is always accessed and written as a unit—regardless of whether the last cells contain any portion of the file. When the system writes this file to disk, the entire 25 memory locations are flushed to disk. In the example, there is nothing located in the

EXHIBIT 4.1 SAMPLE MEMORY BLOCK

T	H	E		E	N	D	$	%	*	M	Y	P	A	S	S	W	O	R	D	=	P	A	S	R

EXHIBIT 4.2 REAL-WORLD EXAMPLE OF MEMORY BLOCK

blocks; however, in a real-world situation, this is highly unlikely. What is more likely is what is shown in Exhibit 4.2.

As a result of the writing operation that the OS does, the RAM slack—everything from the "$" to second "R"—will be written to the hard drive (assuming there is enough file slack on the disk's sector or cluster). By searching the file slack on a system, it is possible to find a number of very valuable bits of information. User passwords, recently accessed documents, image file snippets, and other juicy tidbits of user information all frequently hide in RAM slack and consequently in file slack. Forensic tools can greatly assist investigators by automating, to a great extent, the process of recovering file slack to a readable file. Once the slack has been recovered, it can be read, analyzed, and used just like any other file.

Next investigators search for deleted files. As I explained, most computer operating systems do not really delete files immediately; instead, they "flip a switch" inside the file so that it becomes invisible to the file system, and the computer is tricked into thinking the hard drive real estate is free for use. The beauty of this phenomenon for computer forensic professionals is that the computer's OS does not necessarily write over the recently freed block of memory. Instead, depending on the size and available space on the disk, the next piece of data may be written to an entirely different area of the disk. For investigators, this means that "deleted" files may be recovered. It goes without saying that deleted files can be a very valuable source of evidence.

Using the tools of choice, either a stand-alone tool such as Symantec Corporation's Norton Utilities (www.symantec.com/ index.htm), or a suite of applications such as Encase, investigators search the entire hard drive for deleted files. Once these files are found, the utility programs usually offer investigators a choice of whether to manually rename the file or allow the tool to automate the process. Before proceeding with the recovery of the file, however, it is important to record important data about the file. Things such as access times and other system data can be valuable in identifying who opened the file when.

Whichever alternative investigators choose to recover the file—automated or manual—the result is the same: At the bit level of the hard drive, the "delete" flag is reset so that the system once again recognizes the file and it is rendered accessible.

Although this process is straightforward, problems can arise. As I explained, computers store file information on disk in blocks. These blocks of data are not always full and are not always contiguous. The system might write bits and pieces of a single file across hundreds of different blocks scattered across the suspect's hard drive. This phenomenon leads to disk fragmentation. The more used the disk, the more likely there will be fragmentation. Most computer users are familiar with the Window's utility designed to "defragment" a hard drive. This utility will search a hard drive for file parts that have been scattered across the surface of the disk and will try to reassemble them into a single group of blocks that are contiguous; this can greatly increase file access times.

The fragmentation problem can raise problems for investigators because the system may have overwritten portions of a file that have been fragmented in other areas. If a file has been saved in six sections, for example, that have been scattered across the hard drive, recovering the first section does not guarantee the ability to recover the remaining five. When this problem arises an investigator will find missing addresses and broken file links. All is not necessarily lost; however, the automated process is no longer an option.

Instead, investigators must leapfrog from one address to the next physical address where the file part is alleged to have been stored, often using hexadecimal math and the physical sector addresses assigned to each data block. Following this chain of addresses can lead to recovery of some, none, or all of the missing file parts. Success in this area depends largely on how active the suspect's disk drive has been. Once investigators have searched for and recovered any deleted files, they can be opened, printed, and examined just as any files can.

These procedures are common to nearly every investigation computer forensic examiners undertake. Regardless of the suspected crime, there are bound to be files on the system that have been deleted. Deleted files, however, do not necessarily mean that anything untoward has been going on. In fact, I would venture to guess that every reader's computer currently has a large number of completely benign deleted files floating around on the hard drive.

Yet some things that computer examiners look for are neither common nor benign. One such item is changed file extensions. Although these are easily overlooked by a novice, skilled investigators will quickly identify files that are masquerading as something they are not. All files on a computer system are assigned an extension, the three-digit suffix that appears after the "dot" in a file name. The extension helps the system quickly identify the type of file and then allows the computer to select the appropriate program to access it.

For a file with the extension .bmp, the computer will assume that it contains a bitmapped graphic and will attempt to open it with whichever graphics program is the default program.

Cybercriminals who want to hide the existence of a particular file, perhaps a contraband picture, can change the file's name from "Sheila.bmp," its correct name, to "Sheila.doc." Although the nature of the file has not changed, and it will still open in most graphics applications, casual observers will think the file contains a word processing document and pass right over it during a search.

Computer investigation professionals will not be so careless and will analyze each and every file on the computer to verify they are in fact what they say they are.

Altered file structures are another concern of computer investigators. Whether the suspect has hidden an entire partition or simply made some disk clusters unreadable, forensic investigators are on the lookout for alterations of the disk's geometry. Every computer disk is partitioned into an organized space that is usable by the OS. This process occurs before anything, even an OS, is written to the disk. Depending on the size of the disk, one or more sections, known as partitions, may be created. These partitions are helpful in allowing the OS to organize the files on the computer.

When a disk is divided into more than one partition, there may be several disk drives, known as logical drives, visible to the OS. Although a computer has only one physical hard drive, multiple partitions will function as multiple drives, and the OS will assign successive drive letters to each partition.

Within each partition, the file system subdivides the drive into discrete storage spaces known as clusters. Each cluster is allocated a finite amount of disk real estate and is assigned a specific address. Then, using this addressing system and a permanent copy of this record stored on the disk, the computer OS can gain immediate access to any individual cluster by direct address. The system has grown more efficient over the years, but problems, such as disk failure, can arise.

Even though horror stories abound of catastrophic disk failure, it is more likely for individual clusters and their children, known as sectors, fail. This failure might occur over time, or it could happen because of mechanical failure; more likely still, the drive could have come from the factory defective. When a failure occurs, the information on that particular sector or cluster is unreadable. This results in a read failure and the inability to access the information. This situation is bad enough by itself. However, what if the OS, failing to recognize the cluster as a failed storage unit, writes more, new information into the sector? In order to avoid this, the OS automatically marks individual sectors and clusters as "bad." Once a cluster has been marked as "bad," the disk will no longer recognize it as a usable part of the drive and the read/write heads will pass harmlessly over it. This process ensures smooth operation of disk drives, which routinely are manufactured with a number of bad sectors.

Unfortunately, criminals can use this OS automatic sector marking to their advantage. Using the same tools that forensic technicians use, criminals can manually mark a group of clusters as bad and then manually store files or data in these sectors. Doing this is not exceedingly difficult, but does take some time and know-how. The end result, however, is a totally invisible file, which cannot be seen by the file system and some high-level tools.

For computer investigators, this is really nothing more than a speed bump. Their bit-by-bit examination of the disk examines information at the physical level and will eventually uncover the existence of the data. Hiding files in this way is no match for well-trained and dedicated investigators.

Another scenario in which investigators may encounter hidden information is when the suspect is using a technique known as steganography. Steganography is actually an ancient practice in which clandestine messages were mixed in with a carrier text in order to conceal the existence of the message. Unlike steganography's close relative, cryptography, the message is often open text—although it is possible to encrypt a message and then encode it in a carrier text to avoid detection of the existence of the message itself.

The goal of steganography is not to scramble the message but to hide the existence of the message altogether. In more recent times, computer technology has been harnessed to bring steganography into the digital age. In fact, the digital watermarks commonly used to identify copyright information in graphics files are a form of steganography.

In modern computer steganographic applications, freely available programs are used to insert one file into another. Using complex algorithms, the carrier file—the file into which the concealed file is placed—is altered at the bit level, and individual bits of the concealed file are hidden among them. Because the program changes only every nth bit, the carrier file appears relatively unaltered to the naked eye.

Although nearly any computer file can be used as a carrier file, graphics files are the most popular because they offer a greater amount of overhead in the form of insignificant data bits that can be manipulated. Computer investigators understand this and are always on the lookout for suspicious graphics files—especially if one of the well-known steganography programs is also found on the computer.

Once an encoded file is found, reversing the steganography process without the program's password may be difficult. Although not nearly as robust as that offered by programs such as Pretty Good Protection (PGP; www.pgp.com), the password protection on a stegged program can be daunting. Even though the program often requires a password to reverse the encoding process, often the information is not encrypted. The password may simply be the key to unlock the program and put it in reverse.

Data encryption is a rising problem confronting computer investigators. As computers become more and more powerful, the ability to encrypt data becomes stronger and stronger, but the basic principles used by encryption programs have been around for many years.

For centuries—probably hundreds of centuries—kings and spies have searched for a way to send a secure message to their allies. Encryption allowed them to pass messages to their compatriots without fear that their plans would be uncovered should the message fall into the wrong hands. Computers have not changed this—they have simply made the systems for encryption more powerful.

While the subject of encryption is fodder for entire volumes and relies heavily on very complicated mathematics concepts such as matrix algebra and one-way functions, the principles are simple enough for nonmathematically oriented laypersons such as me to understand. A cryptographic system can be as simple as replacing all instances of the letter a with the letter c. Applied to the message "All dogs have fleas," our encrypted message becomes "Cll dogs hcve flecs." The message is gibberish, but not beyond cracking with a little effort.

Notwithstanding the simplicity of this example, deciphering the message requires some effort on our part. Increase the complexity of our simple substitution algorithm to shift all letters two letters, and our message becomes a little harder to decipher: "Bmm epht ibuf gmfbt." Again, given proper motivation and a few minutes, most people could work through this problem with relative ease. Regardless, as cryptographic systems become more difficult and the keys or algorithms become more complex, solving them without considerable effort—that is, without the key—becomes less likely. If I give you the key to the puzzle, no effort is required to decode it. Computer cryptographic systems operate on the same basic principle except at a much higher level.

Computers have given us the added benefit of efficiency and an ability to carry out staggeringly complex computations nearly instantaneously. Cryptography harnesses this power and manipulates data on the bit level to permanently alter that data, rendering it unreadable—unless you have the key.

Most modern powerful computer encryption systems have keys that allow whoever holds them to unlock the message. Some systems, such as the popular PGP, come with two keys. These two-key solutions in modern encryption solve the age-old problem of protecting the secret because, as you might have guessed, without the key you cannot unlock the message. Therefore, if I want you, my compatriot, to be able to unlock my message, I have to give you the key. This is all well and good when I am in a safe environment, but if I am in a safe environment, I'm less likely to need to encrypt my message.

To solve this problem, programs use advanced mathematic functions based on factorization. In very simple terms, a mathematical algorithm produces two keys, a public key and a private key. These keys—known as asymmetric keys—are related, because they are generated as a pair. The user keeps one key secret—the private key. The other key is published freely. Anyone may access the public key. Using this public key, a message can be encrypted and sent to the holder of the matching private key. Because the two keys in this key pair are related and were mathematically generated, the private key will unlock the message encrypted by the public key. No other key in the world will unlock the message. One of the added benefits of this system is that my public key can be published to everyone, and anyone can send me a secure, encrypted message.

Regardless of how complicated or suspicious it sounds, this method of asymmetric key encryption has been proven to work. As you can see, computers have stepped in to answer the problem of finding a trusted communications channel through which to transfer my key—there is no need to do so, thanks to the asymmetric key cryptography.

When asymmetric key cryptography first appeared on the scene, the computational ability of computers was comparatively quite low. This fact led most scientists to predict that a key pair generated at 128 bits was "unbreakable." However, there has been an exponential growth of computer system power in the years since the first application of these one-way functions to key systems. Technology has grown so rapidly that some cryptography experts are predicting that the ability to "break" this mathematically "unbreakable" algorithm is around the corner. While asymmetric key cryptography remains a theoretically unbreakable system, advances in computer technology may make that statement a historical footnote.

In terms of computer investigations, cryptography poses its own set of challenges. The reality of the scenario facing the computer investigator is this: If a suspect takes enough time to encrypt sensitive data and secures his key in an equally safe storage container, there is very little an investigator can do. At this time, 128-bit asymmetric key encryption is still unbreakable for the average computer investigator. I qualified the last statement because there is speculation that federal agencies responsible for national security have successfully developed a system to break 128-bit encryption. Even if that is true, it is highly unlikely that the local computer crime investigation will be granted access to the resources necessary to break such a key.

Even though today's passwords are practically unbreakable, computer investigators are not totally out of luck. In many cases, there are ways to gain access to encrypted files.

Let us begin with non-128-bit encryption. Fortunately, 128-bit, public/private key encryption is not the only method available. Many proprietary systems exist, and most are quite flimsy and vulnerable to attack. For instance, Windows itself has a password protection scheme that is far from unbreakable. Likewise, most financial programs, such as Money and QuickBooks, have password protection that is far less challenging to break than RSA encryption.[2] In fact, a variety of software programs are designed to crack the password on many popular software products.

If there is no tailor-made software available, investigators might borrow a page from the computer hacker's book and begin a brute-force attack. A brute-force attack is nothing more than systematically attempting to enter every possible combination of letters and numbers until the right combination is discovered by a process of trial and error. It is called brute force because the sheer number of possible number and letter combination in the average eight-digit password is astronomical. Pulling off the attack takes a certain amount of brute computer force.

A variation on the brute-force attack is the dictionary attack. The hacking program begins at the letter *A* and compares every word in the dictionary against the user's password, working its way through the alphabet to *Z*. As you might imagine, this method also takes a tremendous amount of time. A slight variation on this method allows users to customize the dictionary to include proper names and places. This can be a very valuable tool for investigators, who can include in the dictionary names and snippets of personal information about suspects in the hope that they, like most people in the United States, have chosen the name of a loved one, pet, or favorite television character as their password.

Another attack strategy combines more traditional investigative techniques with computer investigation skills. First, investigators attack programs that have relatively weak encryption schemes. Once the program has been broken and the passwords revealed, the investigator begins trying the newly-found password on the more secure programs. This technique depends on human nature and our tendency to reuse the same password for every computer application. As the number of password-protected processes increase, the greater the likelihood that people will reuse passwords. Even if the same password is not reused, often people alter the password by only a few letters or simply add a number to the beginning or end. Either way, investigators have a good starting point for the next method of password cracking.

Even though social engineering is really about tricking people into giving up personal information, I call this method of password cracking social engineering because it relies on human nature in a similar way. In this method, investigators observe the suspect's environment for simple clues that might suggest the password. Some people write down password hints on sticky notes attached to their monitor. Others even put their password on the front page of their day planner under the personal information section. People are creatures of habit; we all do little things that, when considered by trained investigators, may lead to a bigger picture—and that bigger picture could be the keys to the kingdom.

Finally, when all else fails, investigators have been known to request a password from suspects themselves. Notwithstanding the necessary cautions about Miranda warnings and legal concerns over compelled answers, suspects sometimes opt to cooperate in the hope that their equipment will be spared. Whatever the motivation, good investigators never overlook all the possibilities.

CONCLUSION

This chapter has barely scratched the surface of the analysis of digital evidence; however, it should help you to form a clearer picture of what the analysis of a computer system involves. In this overview, I have not discussed what investigators do when confronted with damaged files or how they can identify unknown file formats. Although all these issues are very real concerns for field investigators, space constraints preclude my discussing them here. The contents of this chapter should serve as a starting point from which you can explore further.

In the next chapter, we turn our attention to the role that investigators play after the last byte of information has been analyzed. Although not as full of pitfalls as the seizure process, and less taxing than the analysis of the evidence, this process also brings with it some very challenging obstacles.

NOTES

1. As you may recall, as soon as the investigator recovers the original evidence using a disk imaging program, she must make a working

copy. As such, all analysis is being done on a copy of the copied image.

2. RSA is an acronym for the last names of Ron Rivest, Adi Shamir, and Len Adleman, who were the MIT researchers who first described the algorithm in 1977

SUGGESTED READING

Brown, Christopher L. T. *Computer Evidence: Collection & Preservation.* Hingham, MA: Charles River Media, 2006.

Kruse, Warren G., and Jay G. Heiser. *Computer Forensics: Incident Response Essentials.* Boston: Addison-Wesley, 2002.

Nelson, Bill, Amelia Phillips, Frank Enfinger, and Christopher Steuart. *Guide to Computer Forensics and Investigations*, 2nd ed. Boston: Thomson-Course Technology, 2006.

Vacca, John R. *Computer Forensics: Computer Crime Scene Investigation.* Hingham, MA: Charles River Media, 2002.

5

REPORTING AND RENDERING THE OPINION

INTRODUCTION

With the heavy lifting of collection, analysis, and reconstruction now complete, computer forensic experts must now turn their attention to reporting on their findings. Many times, regardless of how proficient or skilled investigators are, ultimately the success of the case will revolve around how well they handle this stage of the process.

The axiom that a job is not finished until the paperwork is complete is equally true in the world of computer forensic investigation—perhaps more so. Regardless of how well investigators comb through the digital evidence, or how damaging to the opposition's case the information they find is, it will be valueless unless the results can be conveyed to the appropriate people in a concise and coherent way. Computer forensic investigators may not be experienced with this step.

In this chapter, I explain some of the requirements investigators are forced to confront, such as effective presentation and proper documentation. Even in cases that investigators view as being "in-house" or nonprosecutorial, taking the necessary steps to ensure evidentiary admissibility is extremely important. If investigators do this, they prepare the case for every possibility. When the nature of the case changes, and the strictly administrative investigation suddenly becomes a wrongful termination lawsuit, there are fewer loose ends that need tidying up.

PREPARING THE REPORT

After having spent nearly two decades in law enforcement, I can safely say a few things without hesitation. One is that investigators really hate report writing. Regardless of how well investigators write, or how important the case is, the paperwork facet of the investigation always seems to be neglected. Even though this fact is inevitable, it is something that must be overcome in order to pursue a case properly.

Documentation of the investigation begins well before the report is written. In fact, as I have discussed, investigators must begin documenting everything from the moment the case begins until the final piece of evidence has been processed and safely stored away.

Documentation, whether photographic or written, will be the framework from which the final report and findings will emerge. Therefore, it is crucial to get it right the first time.

Photographic Documentation

From the moment investigators arrive at the scene of the seizure, they must begin documenting, photographically, every aspect of the computer setup. In combination with the sketches investigators do at the scene, these photographs will help them to accurately reconstruct the computer installation six months later when the case is finally being prepared for presentation. Even the most basic computer configuration can be difficult to reconstruct without diligent documentation at the time it is seized.

Investigators must take special care to make sure that every wire, cable, and connector is properly documented. Investigators must include data on both where they originate and where they terminate. Labels, tape, and wire-tires help to clearly and accurately identify each component and its purpose.

Even in cases where litigation is unlikely, proper documentation can help investigators figure out exactly what is going on in a given computer environment.

As you might expect, the larger the computer installation grows, the more complicated it is to disassemble. Reassembly can be impossible unless thorough documentation precedes the very first keystroke, cable disconnect, or power-down.

Earlier we discussed the fact that investigators often must make decisions on the fly, evaluating the best way to attack an installation for investigation. Sometimes the system will be running; other times it will not. Sometimes investigators can decide in advance whether to attempt a live collection of volatile data such as user logs, currently running processes, and event logs. Other times this choice will be made on site. When investigators decide to attempt a live collection—in other words, to obtain evidence from a running computer system—step-by-step documentation will help them to reconstruct the status of the system at the time it was seized.

In other cases, the decision to shut down a system before collecting the evidence will be the more appropriate choice. In those cases, documentation must include things such as photographs of the screen showing all the programs that are running at the time and any users who might be logged in. In either scenario, properly recording the state of the system before investigator interaction is crucial. As I have cautioned, the mere movement of a mouse or tap of a keystroke will irrevocably alter the system. This alteration, while not necessarily fatal, must definitely be documented.

An accurate sketch of the scene goes hand in hand with the photographic documentation. Even though photographs really are worth 1,000 words, carefully rendered sketches that show distances, configurations, and cable routing schematics can clarify distortions that are inevitable when projecting a three-dimensional surface onto a two-dimensional plane like a photograph. As the system is being disassembled, computer investigators need to list each item that is being disconnected, where it came from, and where it is going to.

Although the scene sketch need not be a work of fine art, it must be accurate. Measurements, where necessary, should be accurate and should give future investigators or opposing counsel's experts the ability to reconstruct the scene exactly as original investigators found it. The computer installation is the crime scene, no different from the scene of a murder or a burglary. Investigators must document how the suspected criminal left the computer, just as they would document a murder scene.

Reporting

The on-scene documentation is really just the beginning. Investigators must continue the documentation process throughout the entire investigation. Every action of investigators must be based on sound logic and be documented. The steps taken to power up, collect data from, and image a computer are all areas on which opposing counsel, or hired-gun experts, will launch an attack. Step-by-step documentation makes defense much easier.

For investigators using forensic suites such as FTK and Encase, powerful reporting functionality is built in. During every stage of the computer analysis, these tools record every action and can export the actual data collected from the computer hard drive into a report, making cross-referencing and including exhibits in the report almost as simple as point-and-click.

Regardless of the way investigators document the flow of the investigation, all reports should have certain sections. The order in which these sections appear will be different from report to report, but they are important to provide outsiders will all the information necessary to comprehend what the investigation has uncovered.

Executive Summary or Abstract

If a report is long, and most computer forensic analysis reports are, it may be helpful to include an abstract that provides the basic facts and an overview of the steps and findings. This summary should be concise, no more than two or three paragraphs, and should convey all the essential facts to the reader.

Table of Contents

Again, long reports will have multiple sections. Breaking the information into related sections can help create an organized and easy-to-follow document. The table of contents provides a roadmap for busy readers to "fast forward" to the point in the report that contains the information that is of the most interest to them.

Body or Findings

The heart of the report is the findings section. Here investigators outline the results of the case. This section may also include subparts, such as an introduction, methods review, and discussion of procedures used. It also can include restatements of questions to be answered and relevant facts that may have influenced particular procedures.

Conclusion

This section is where investigators render an opinion, if one is warranted. Here investigators answer questions and convey the actual results of the analysis.

Supporting Documents

This section can consist of subparts that provide other materials that investigators referred to or used during the investigation. On a lengthy or complicated investigation, investigators may refer to outside reference sources, such as hardware and software manuals for products analyzed. For example, when analyzing a computer system running proprietary accounting software, investigators might be unfamiliar with the program processes and flow. In that case, investigators will use the software manuals to determine what the software was supposed to do and whether anything out of the ordinary was occurring. Attaching these manuals, or excerpts, may be helpful to the reader.

Likewise, depending on the complexity of the case, investigators may include a glossary or list of terms to help readers understand technical terms used in the report. Regardless of how sophisticated investigators are, readers of the report may be barely computer literate. As a result, the language of the report might be beyond their comprehension. Although investigators should strive to make sure the report is easy to read by the average reader, some use of technical jargon and specific computer terms is necessary. A glossary or list of terms relieves readers from having to search outside sources for definitions.

Appendixes

The appendix section might be omitted on some reports. On others, it might be longer than the preceding sections combined. An appendix can contain logs, particularly important exhibits, or images from the computer and other miscellaneous supporting documents that will enable readers to interpret the report more easily.

The investigators' curricula vitae (CVs) are of particular interest. A CV is a detailed résumé that includes education, publications, relevant experience, and professional affiliations that investigators possess that will help to establish their status as experts. In fact, under the Federal Rules of Evidence, an investigator's CV may be required as part of the discovery process. Attaching it to the report ensures that whoever is responsible for preparing the case for future legal action will have all the necessary bona fides on the investigator.

PRESENTATION

Once the investigative report or summary of findings is complete, often the next step is presentation. Normally, computer forensic experts only undertake analyses at the request of a third party. Whether the third party is a private lawyer, prosecuting attorney, private citizen—in the case of a police department—or perhaps the compliance arm of a corporate entity, the decision to begin an investigation lies outside an investigator's purview. For this reason, once the investigation has begun, investigators are ultimately answerable to someone and at some point in time must convey the outcome of the investigation to interested third parties. Ultimately, the report will form the basis of this accountability, and will used in two major ways.

First, the report may serve as an internal document. In this case, investigators forward the report through channels, at which time whatever internal action is deemed necessary is instituted. In the second scenario, the report forms the basis for further legal action.

Further legal action can include action by government agencies, such as the Equal Employment Opportunity Commission, the Environmental Protection Agency, or Federal Communications Commission, to list only a few. It could also take the form of prosecution under state and federal laws, or it could be a civil action instituted by private individuals. Regardless of the form of the legal action, the report will provide the foundation for what comes next.

The rules of evidence and trial procedures play a major role in the flow of the case in a legal action. The next section provides an overview of the trial process in both civil and criminal actions. Then I provide some information about which rules of evidence come into play most often and how they might impact the testimony of computer forensic specialists. Last, I cover the role that computer forensic specialists, as experts, play in the trial process.

TRIAL PROCESS

Regardless of whether the case is a civil action or a criminal prosecution, the organization and flow are fairly similar. Each has particular facets that are unique, but the rules and procedures are fairly consistent. It may help to think of the trial process in three steps: pretrial, trial, and posttrial. Here I discuss the civil litigation process, commenting on the way in which the criminal process differs.

Dispute

Every case begins with a dispute. Whether the disagreement is over one party's failure to perform under a contract or arises because of someone's failure to exercise due care, the dispute sets the litigation process in motion. Likewise, in the criminal system, the case begins with an offense.

Both the criminal and civil systems address wrongdoing. In some cases, they address the *same* wrongdoing. An example of this is the O. J. Simpson case. O. J. Simpson was prosecuted in both the criminal system and civil court. He was acquitted in the criminal trial but was found liable in the civil trial. This is possible because the two different systems have different goals. The system of criminal prosecution is in place to address public wrongs—those offenses that are considered by the majority to be so at risk of disrupting the fabric of the social contract that the government should be responsible for punishing them. The civil system, however, is in place to address private wrongs.

Private wrongs are those things that involve intimate and personal behavior between people. These wrongs include things like contracts and how we order our daily lives. In some cases, private wrongs occur in the public sphere. Killing someone, while in some regard a private matter between the victim and the perpetrator, is also on the list of those things that we view as disruptive to the public order. As a result, remedies are available in both systems simultaneously.

The divergent verdicts in the Simpson case can be directly attributed to the burden of proof that is required in the respective systems. In most civil cases, the person who is bringing forward the action must prove his or her entitlement to prevail by a level of proof known as the preponderance of evidence. Although artificial numeric values are often assigned to the levels of proof, converting fluid concepts like this into hard numerical values is tough. Many practitioners will explain preponderance of evidence standard as the more-likely-than-not standard.

Conversely, in the criminal system, the standard to which the prosecution (the criminal plaintiff) must prove the case is known as the reasonable doubt standard—a concept sometimes even more difficult to understand than the preponderance of evidence standard. Regardless of how you define reasonable doubt, it is a standard that requires far more proof and much weightier evidence to reach. As a result, it is perfectly understandable for two different verdicts to flow from the same set of facts. In the O. J. Simpson case, the district attorney's office was unable—for whatever reason—to convince the jury beyond a reasonable doubt that the defendant had committed murder.

In the civil case, the plaintiffs, however, needed only to show that it was more likely than not that O. J. Simpson was responsible for the wrongful deaths of Nicole Brown Simpson and Ron Goldman. This lower standard of proof explains why two different results flowed from the same basic facts.

Therefore, these two systems coexist alongside one another and often overlap. For investigators, this overlap means that it is possible that two different burdens and two different sets of rules will govern the evidentiary process.

Even though a dispute is present in all legal cases, the existence of a dispute does not automatically ensure there will be a trial. In fact, computer investigators might even be valuable tools in avoiding a trial. During the precharging phase of a case, where investigation and fact finding are going on in earnest, negotiations are often happening simultaneously. Sometimes these negotiations are fueled to one degree or another by what each side feels confident about in terms of proof. Computer investigators often can shed some light on exactly what each side can hope to prove. As a result, one or both parties might be favorably inclined to reach a pretrial settlement. When these precharging negotiations fail, the formal legal process begins.

Complaint

Each case must begin with a charging document, which frames the basic issues the parties will argue about. In a civil case, the charging document is called the pleading, or the complaint. The complaint states the names of the parties, the basis for the action—both factual and legal—and the relief sought.

In the criminal case, the charging document takes the form of an information or an indictment setting forth the exact criminal act or acts the defendant is accused of committing. Both types of charging documents have very specific requirements as to their form and what they must include, and often have minor variations among differing jurisdictions.

Once the initiating party, known as the plaintiff in the civil system, files the pleadings, the defendant—the person accused of the wrongdoing—must be notified that he or she is being sued. Even if extensive negotiations between the two parties have been going on for months, the notification requirement is a very strict legal requirement. Without proper notification, the court will lack the authority to hear that particular case. Notification is also called service of process.

Service of Process

Service of process is nothing more than official notification by the court to defendants that they are required to appear and answer the charges outlined in the complaint. This very formal procedure ensures that defendants are made aware of the exact charges, and serves as the basis for the next document in the flow of the case: the responsorial pleading, also commonly called the answer.

In a criminal case, the functional equivalent to the service of process is the arrest and arraignment. In the civil system, the ultimate punishment for a finding of legal responsibility is forfeiture of money—a civil judgment. In the criminal justice system, a finding of legal responsibility—guilt—can result in forfeiture of freedom. Our legal system draws a bright-line distinction between these two principles. As a result, in circumstances where the accused is facing possible forfeiture of freedom, our system requires extra measures to ensure that only those most deserving of such deprivation are sentenced to it. The burden of proof in criminal cases is one such safeguard. As you explore the differences between the two court systems, it might be helpful to keep the ultimate punishments—with their different levels of protection—in mind. Our inherited reverence for human freedom explains many things. The process of arraignment and first appearance is one.

The civil service of process is essentially all that is required to start the civil adversarial process. More is required in the criminal process: The system must inform defendants explicitly what they are accused of and what their rights are. The first appearance, arraignment, and preliminary hearing stages of the criminal process are all safeguards that have been added to our criminal system to ensure that defendants are properly informed of exactly what they stand to lose.

Once the formal charging has occurred, the official pretrial process begins. Technically, everything leading up to the trial itself is considered pretrial, but in reality, often only those things that happen after charging are considered part of the pretrial phase.

Pretrial

In most cases, the lion's share of the work is done during this pretrial phase. During pretrial, the role of computer investigators becomes even more important.

Pretrial activities include motion filings, depositions and interrogatories, and demands for production. The discovery process allows both sides to assess strengths in their own case and probe for the weaknesses of their opponents. This parry and thrust may at first seem counterintuitive to an adversarial system such as our own; however, the underlying goal of our system—truth seeking—supports it.

Even though a free exchange of information between both sides is the concept, the implementation often falls short. Either side may legally withhold from the opponent a number of things, such as attorney-client privileged information, attorney-work product, and other sensitive information, but the general rule requires disclosure of nearly every aspect of the case. The rules of discovery often impact computer forensic experts directly.

In some ways, the degree of impact depends on whether the case is moving forward in the federal or a state system, as these systems have slightly different rules of pretrial discovery. Nevertheless, both sides require very specific disclosures when expert witnesses are involved. Computer forensic technicians are most likely to be called in their capacity as experts, not lay witnesses. The distinction between the two is very important, because it will dictate exactly what witnesses will be allowed to testify to.

Both the federal and state legal systems have very specific rules regarding witness testimony, and generally speaking, there are two categories: experts and lay witnesses. Lay witnesses might be the type of witness the average reader is familiar with. These witnesses are those who will testify the light was green at the time the car entered the intersection or that the defendant had a gun in his waistband. These types of witnesses can testify only on factual information within their personal experience. In other words, they can testify only to facts that they personally observed or experienced. Experts, however, can testify to opinions. But before they can testify to their opinion, several things must occur. The first is disclosure during pretrial discovery.

In general, all rules of procedure, both civil and criminal, require notification of the opposing side that a party intends to use expert witnesses. Under most circumstances, the rules go so far as to require production of a report detailing exactly what experts will testify to. Then, prior to witnesses actually being allowed to offer an opinion, the process of voir dire, where witnesses are thoroughly examined not about the facts of the case but about individual qualifications to testify will determine whether the jury will hear the experts' opinions. While the voir dire process usually occurs once the trial has started, the pretrial phase is often the point where computer forensic witnesses must defend their actions and establish their credentials.

During this phase, each side tries to collect information about the opponent's case through depositions and interrogatories. Of these, depositions are probably the more frequent situations for expert witnesses. A deposition is a formal question-and-answer session in which one or both sides has the opportunity to ask practically any questions of a witness they want. The witness's testimony is recorded under oath, and may serve as the basis for future impeachment; more important, it serves as an investigative tool for the attorneys.

Even though formal rules dictate the conduct of depositions, many times they are very intimidating because they are often the only chance opposing counsel will get to size up a witness. As such, most attorneys will use the deposition setting to find witness weaknesses, hot buttons, and potential chinks in the armor of the opponent's case. The fact-finding nature of the deposition supports this mission nicely, and the rules of procedure lay a fairly wide berth through which the attorneys can navigate. In general, the rules of relevance and materiality hold little sway in the deposition. Instead, because of the fact-finding nature of depositions, the only benchmark of proper questioning is whether it could lead to discovery of new, relevant evidence.

Objections as to relevance, or any evidentiary objections for that matter, are rarely an option, and generally speaking, no questions are truly out of bounds. As you might imagine, this free-for-all concept can lead to abuse.

In the long run, though, the notion that truth is the ultimate goal of our justice system supports this liberal view of discovery. After all, the case should be decided based on the facts, not on who was more able to keep their evidence a secret. The job of discovery is to avoid situations of trial by ambush.

Once the pretrial discovery process is complete, and assuming that both sides have rejected settlements or plea offers, the trial proper can begin.

Trial

In the criminal justice system, the trial is actually the exception to the rule. In fact, very few cases, comparatively speaking, ever go to trial. Most are disposed of through a plea agreement. As distasteful as this is to some, it is a necessary evil in our already overburdened criminal justice system. Likewise, in our similarly overburdened civil system, many cases never set foot inside the courtroom. Instead, settlements, often on the eve of trial, offer a compromise between the parties in which neither side must risk the burdens of a trial. Assuming that no pleas or settlements are possible, the trial will move forward.

In the trial phase itself, there is an orderly flow to the process. Exhibit 5.1 lists the normal phases of a trial. The civil process is on the left, the criminal process is on the right. You can see that there are considerable similarities between the two.

These steps, while abbreviated in some trials and expanded in others, are present in every case. Computer forensic experts play a role in each. For example, during the jury selection phase, experts may serve as jury

Civil Trial	Criminal Trial
Jury Selection (if necessary)	Jury Selection (if necessary)
Opening Statements	Opening Statements
Plaintiff's Case	Prosecution/State's case
Defendant's Case	Defendant's Case
Closing arguments	Closing arguments
Verdict	Verdict
Damages phase (if necessary)	Sentencing
Post trial motions	Post trial motions

EXHIBIT 5.1 PHASES OF CIVIL AND CRIMINAL TRIALS

consultants, helping counsel to size up the likelihood that the complicated computer evidence will be well received by jury members.

Computer forensic experts can also assist in the preparation of opening statements by helping to frame complicated computer concepts into more jury-palatable jargon. The role of experts in the plaintiffs' and the defendants' cases are obvious. As expert witnesses, they will be rendering opinions that are intended to help the jury reach a favorable verdict. In the damages phase, computer experts can offer testimony as to amount of loss, which may determine the actual recovery amount for the prevailing party.

Regardless of which side has retained computer experts, their testimony and input will be crucial at all stages of the case. Not only will their testimony be important, but during the pretrial or even the pre-filing stage, experts can help to shape the entire nature of the case. A well-trained computer forensic expert often can change the overall game plan of both sides by bringing to light issues that are pivotal to the outcome.

It is clear that computer forensic experts are valuable at all stages of both civil and criminal cases. Yet the most visible role experts play is often the one that is most difficult to pull off: that of testimonial experts.

Testimonial experts are present in every type of case. The success of many criminal cases rests on the testimony of experts in fields, such as fingerprinting, DNA, and forensic accounting. Likewise, in civil cases, forensic accountants often render valuable opinions on valuation, negligence, or due diligence. Medical experts are ubiquitous in malpractice cases; a product liability case without the presence of at least one engineering or design expert would hardly be a case at all. In summary, most experts are called on to offer live testimony in court. Unfortunately, experts do not always make the best witnesses.

Regardless of their qualifications in their field, experts must, above all, be skilled at communicating their information to the jury. It is a given that if the expert is appearing in court, she has passed the threshold level of expertise outlined by the *Daubert v. Merrill Dow* case (509 U.S. 579 [1993]) and is considered a qualified expert in a recognized field. What is not as assured is the expert's ability to connect with the jury.

A significant portion of the trial process has a foundation in the dramatic. Regardless of whether attorneys will readily admit it or not, trials are largely well-scripted, well-rehearsed dramas in which a flair for the dramatic and the timing, pacing, and delivery of a polished actor are highly valuable. Delivering the required information to a jury in a captivating way is a learned art. Successful trial lawyers have learned this art through many years of practice.

Expert witnesses do not necessarily readily grasp the necessity of being captivating. Many computer forensic experts believe that delivering the facts in a precise, concise way is all that is required. The truth is that experts are witnesses for one reason—because they understand concepts that the rest of us have trouble grasping in depth. For this reason, unless it is carefully delivered, expert testimony can be dry and boring, and could lead to greater confusion on the part of the jury. Recognizing this tendency, many attorneys have taken to employing techniques formerly reserved for the stage in the court room. Aside from the obvious ethical issues that arise, injecting a component of performance makes the attorney's job more difficult. Getting experts to think this way is sometimes even more difficult.

Even if computer forensic experts do not feel comfortable thinking of their role in the courtroom as that of actors in a drama, it is still important that they view their job as being about communication. In order to communicate clearly and effectively to laypeople, computer forensic experts must develop a new set of skills, including communication, presentation, and persuasion.

Many books offer advice to experts on how to approach their testimony role. I will not add to them by recounting how to testify. Instead, I refer the interested reader to one of these books, including *Forensic Accounting and Fraud Investigation for Non-Experts,* which I cowrote with Howard Silverstone. It dedicates several chapters to the role that the testimonial expert plays in the courtroom.

CONCLUSION

As with most things in life, a job well done requires seeing it through to the end. In the case of a computer forensic examination, experts must have the perseverance to stay on task until the final juror has been polled. Although this might appear obvious, it is something that scientific experts often overlook. Their fixation on the pure science may overshadow the need to effectively communicate the results of their analysis in a way that the average person can understand. When experts overlook the communication and reporting stages of their job, the result is total negation of the reason they were retained in the first place: a successful conclusion of a legal dispute.

In this chapter, I have introduced you to the presentation aspect of the computer forensic investigators' role. By now you should have a much better understanding of the role that computer forensic experts play in an investigation as well as a better understanding of the nature and flow of an investigation itself. Building on this information, future chapters will take a look at what computer crime really is.

SUGGESTED READING

Gardner, Thomas. J, and Terry M. Anderson. *Criminal Evidence Principles and Cases*, 6th ed. Belmont, CA: Thomson Wadsworth, 2007.

Neubauer, D. W. *America's Court and the Criminal Justice System*, 8th ed. Belmont, CA: Thomson Wadsworth, 2005.

Samaha, Joel. *Criminal Procedure*, 6th ed. Belmont, CA: Thomson-Wadsworth, 2005.

Silverstone, Howard, and Michael Sheetz. *Forensic Accounting and Fraud Investigation for Non-Experts*. Hoboken, NJ: John Wiley & Sons, 2004.

6

COMPUTER ATTACKS

HACKERS AND PHREAKZ OH MY

When average people hear the phrase "computer crime," their thoughts usually turn to images of loner teens perched in front of a computer terminal, its sickening glow illuminating their pimpled faces as they peck away at the keyboard searching for illusive backdoor entrances to CIA databases and Department of Defense main frames. Although those images do exist as one component of modern computer crime, there are other facets to this ever-evolving world.

Earlier we explored the world of computer forensic experts—what they do and do not do. In this chapter and those that follow, we are going to turn our attention more to whom computer forensic investigators are likely to run up against. In this motley assortment of adversaries, they are as likely to encounter a banker as they are a pimply-faced overachiever. As computers have evolved, so have those who employ them for evil.

The more omnipresent the computer has become, the more mainstream its application to criminal activity have become. In the next few chapters we will look at several aspects of computer crime. We begin by looking at crimes that attack computers from the outside, followed by crimes and the criminals who attack computers from the inside, and finally we look at some ways in which the changes in computer technology have thrust them into all facets of criminal activity—no longer are they the sole province of "geeks and phreakz."

HACKERS: UNAUTHORIZED USE AND TRESPASSING

The evolution of computer technology and the Internet has played a pivotal role in the development of the computer criminal. Computer hackers have matured from the original "knowledge-seeking" explorer depicted in the "Hacker Manifesto, " to full-on marauding, pillaging digital rapists whose mission is to seek and destroy information.

Although traditional benign hackers whose overactive curiosity and misplaced allegiance to an altruistic code of honor still exist, they seem to have taken a backseat to modern malicious computer criminals whose motive is profit and destruction. Hacking and phreaking have a long and, some would say, romantic history.

The term "hacker" has long been associated with computer criminals. In reality, the term had a much more innocuous meaning originally, as a compliment. Hackers were highly skilled computer programmers who were able to creatively and innovatively find programming methods around very difficult problems.[1] Being labeled a hacker within the computer programming community was perhaps the highest form of compliment that one could receive.

However, the more pejorative definition—a person who attempts to compromise the integrity of a computer system without authorization—has become the more widely used and popular one. The emergence of computer hackers in the pre-Internet days of computers gave rise to a second term: phreaker. While the derivation of the term is subject to dispute, some believe that it is the combination of the words "phone" and "freq," which is short for "frequency."[2]

Phreaking, in the early days, often went hand in hand with hacking—so much so that most times the community itself was referred to as the hacking-phreaking community. The reason for this close association is largely the cost of long-distance phone calls.

As I explained earlier, in the days before the Internet, all computer connections with remote terminals were made using telephone lines and dial-up modems. Advances such as DSL, cable modems, and T-1—high bandwidth communication lines—accounts were merely pipe dreams at the time. Because long-distance telephone calls incurred per-minute charges, slow 28.8 baud connections could easily cost hackers $1,000 monthly phone bills.

To overcome this financial limitation to their exploration, hackers began to adopt a discovery made early on regarding the operation of frequency-switched telephone equipment—the 2600 hertz (Hz) frequency could garner a free telephone call.

In other words, anyone who could replicate the signals of a 2600 Hz frequency could fool the telephone company's central office into granting long-distance access, without the need for a coin deposit. This discovery was made by a group of individuals; however, the names of Joe Engressia and

John "Captain Crunch" Draper are often linked with the implementation of this phenomenon known as phreaking.[3]

Humble in its beginnings, the phreaking phenomenon soon grew, and relatively unsophisticated devices known as blue boxes began to show up in hackers' toolkits. This tool, named for the color of the plastic kit box, was easily assembled by someone of average electronics kit building skill from a handful of parts found at the local Radio Shack. Smaller in size than the average book, a blue box allowed hackers to interface with the telephone and input the proper audio signals to fool the phone company's in-band signaling equipment and get nearly unlimited telephone access—a godsend for the average hacker.

This phreaking craze became so popular, and the relationship between hacking and phone phreaking so solid, that an underground organization began to develop. The birth of the publication *2600: The Hacker's Quarterly* signaled the strength that this counterculture had realized. Begun in 1984, *The Hacker's Quarterly* is still in publication. Reachable online at www.2600.com, it has gone mainstream and is available at major newsstands. It has become a reliable source for "white hat" hackers (computer professionals who test and probe computer system security to identify weaknesses, not to exploit them but to help the owners patch them).

During the hacker-phreaker era of the 1970's and 80's, an underground culture developed, and the Legion of Doom, Cult of the Dead Cow, and Masters of Deception became household names among hackers. Guided by their misdirected belief that information wants to be free, these groups attacked countless computer systems and, if nothing else, raised awareness of computer vulnerability to a new level.[4]

Among the contributions that hacker groups made to our culture, war dialing is one of the best known. Popularized by the 1983 film *Wargames,* war dialing was a potent tool in the hacker's tool belt. In fact, my first encounter with the hacker world involved war dialing.

As you may recall from Chapter 1, the young hacker I first encountered many years ago had a stack of papers in his backpack. This stack of papers was the printout from his war dialing program, Demon Dialer. In war dialing, users program their computers to sequentially dial every possible combination of telephone numbers in a given prefix and identify those with computers attached. Hackers often initiate war dialing in the early stages of an attack to identify potential targets. They set the war dialing program to search the programmed prefix overnight. In the morning, well-rested hackers, armed with the printout from the war dialer, attempt to access all the modem lines on the list.

With the rise of the Internet, traditional hacking and phreaking techniques have become less popular, and new forms of computer attack have evolved. Although some diehard phreakers continue to tinker with traditional phone-line attacks, the Internet has offered hackers a new world to explore.

As computers have evolved, a stratification of the hacker world has occurred. Experts have loosely divided hackers by outlook or skill level.

Black hat hackers are those who attack and disable computer systems for personal fulfillment or gain. These are the quintessential hackers who are responsible for the denials of service, data security compromises, and hundreds of thousands of dollars a year in losses. These hackers are motivated purely by profit or destruction. The computer security industry is perhaps the only group of people who can benefit from their activities.[5]

White hat hackers attack and attempt to compromise computer systems, like black hatters, but for a different reason. Unlike black hatters, who ply their trade with evil intent, white hatters use their tools for good. Even though they attempt to gain unauthorized access to computer systems, once they are successful, they immediately notify the computer system administrator of the system's vulnerability. In some circumstances, white hatters may even work for the administrator as a sort of consultant to help them probe for weaknesses in their system. In fact, the 1992 movie *Sneakers* had a plot line that loosely followed a set of white hat hackers as they test security systems. While the movie has its share of Hollywood hype, the depiction of this role that white hatters play in security system testing is accurate.[6]

Gray hat hackers are a blend of the black hat and the white hat categories. Not entirely evil, gray hat hackers often probe security systems for weaknesses. When they find them, unlike the white hatters, who notify the administrator immediately, gray hatters might extort the owner or hold the information for ransom. Another way in which gray hat hackers profit from their hacking activity is by identifying the security vulnerability, then recommending that the system administrator hire one of the hacker's associates.[7]

Script kiddies is a derisive term used by more skilled hackers to refer to hackers who may not know the underlying basis for the exploit but simply deploy a script (a small, self-contained computer program that allows them to gain access to a particular system), which does the work. Script kiddies rarely possess superior computer programming skill, in contrast with their predecessors, and spend most of their time surfing the Internet, downloading the latest scripts. To many experts, script kiddies are a more dangerous threat to computer security than even black hat hackers.

As the computer community has evolved and computer technology has made it possible for users to know less and less about the actual workings of the technology, the hacking community has experienced the same phenomenon.[8] In the early days of hacking, legends like Mark Abene, known among the hacker community as Phiber Optik and a founding member of the Masters of Deception, and Chris Goggans, aka Erik Bloodaxe of Legion of Doom fame, were highly skilled technical experts in computers and telephone switching systems. Many of their exploits (computer compromises) were done through hours of trial and error and supported by an often-encyclopedic knowledge of the systems themselves.[9] Today's generation of hacker kids are less computer literate and rely on scripts that automatically attack the vulnerabilities of systems.

In general, black hat attacks are very narrowly limited and executed by computer programmers with a high level of skill. Although theft and data compromise are often their goal, their attack is usually surgical in nature. Script kiddies, however, are unskilled practitioners who deploy code snippets into systems with no real idea of what may happen. They have far less system knowledge than black hatters, and unintentional, irreparable devastation may result from their exploits.

Hactivists are people who use computer technology for social protest and civil disobedience. Incidents of hactivism span the range of computer hacking, from crashing Web sites of politically incorrect targets to disabling censorship software on government computers.[10] Although many experts group hactivists into one of the previous groups, the continued growth of computers as tools of political statement clearly justifies a category of its own.

Cyberterrorists make up the final group that has emerged relatively recently. Although terrorism has long been a problem of international proportion, only fairly recently have experts acknowledged that computer hackers who may compromise certain elements of our critical infrastructure may pose a significant threat to public safety and cause widespread injuries. Acts of cyberterrorism include things such as accessing and disabling entire power grids, telephone networks, nuclear power facilities, and emergency communications networks.[11]

Opinion is divided as to the real threat to public health, but a controlled experiment conducted by the National Security Agency (NSA) revealed that there are significant cyberterrorism risks, at least in theory. For example, the NSA experiment proved that it was possible to bring down the power grids in Los Angeles, Chicago, Washington, and New York, causing massive power failure. The Department of Defense (DOD) computer services, including e-mail, telephones, and databases, were shut down simultaneously.

Perhaps most frightening was the ability of DOD hackers, in another controlled experiment, to gain unauthorized control of the DOD computer and effect a mock crash of a commercial airliner.[12]

All of these attacks, while mere simulations, were replications of real-world possibilities that could disable, at least temporarily, many of our most vital resources. As our nation becomes more and more dependent on computer technology, we may become more and more vulnerable to computer attack. Therefore, this new category of hacker is of growing concern. In addition, with the rise of worldwide terror organizations, the demographic makeup of the cyberterrorist is likely to be different from the traditional hacker. Although the profile of the typical computer hacker has changed only somewhat over the past 30 years, the cyberterrorist is much more likely to be affiliated with traditional terror organizations and have strong computer skills.

WIRELESS HACKING

Within the past 10 years, wireless technology has moved from the realm of new technology to ubiquitous. Businesses, seeking to improve efficiency, increase their network architecture, and provide workers with 24/7 connectivity, have followed the steady march toward wireless networking. Likewise, homeowners have climbed on board and added fuel to the fire of rapidly expanding wireless installations.

Like hard-wired networks, wireless networks allow users to connect to a central computer network, with the added advantage of no cumbersome computer cables. In the short term, this solution is cost effective, allowing companies to reduce installation costs and increase worker productivity and efficiency. In the long term, however, wireless technology may have some added costs. One of these costs comes in the form of added security threats.

Wireless networks require no physical connection to the network. Whereas the traditional company local area network (LAN) required users to tether themselves to a central backbone, the wireless user can connect from anywhere in the office where the wireless signal can be received. In the wired environment, controlling access to the hardware is fairly straightforward. Connecting to the LAN requires presence in the building and access to a physical network connection

Most readers are familiar with the process of plugging a laptop in to an RJ-45 cable connector in order to gain access to a company network. The wireless network removes the requirement of physical connectivity and replaces it with radiowave connectivity. Instead of physically plugging in to the system, the wireless user's laptop connects to the physical appearance point through radio transmissions. Even though the appearance point is still inside the secured space of the office environment, the laptop does not have to be. In fact, the wireless-enabled computer can connect to an appearance point anywhere within the transmit-and-receive distance of a particular appearance point.

The inability to control the location from which users log on to the appearance point is at the heart of the security problem in a wireless environment. Wireless networks attempt to overcome this weakness through encryption and access verification. When enabled, wireless network verification processes work very similarly to authentication and verification procedures in a wired environment. Users must supply a username and password in order to gain access to the network. In theory, this is a good solution, and challenge/response authentication has been an acceptable form of access control for many years.

However, the implementation of the authentication process, at least in the earlier networks running under the 802.11b protocol,[13] fell short of truly secure protection. The communications protocol that was developed for wireless networks, known as the 802.11 standard, has built-in protection; however, this protection scheme is less robust than it should be. Sparing you the nitty-gritty details of the algorithms and their weaknesses, the primary concern is that, unlike the encryption algorithms discussed in earlier chapters, the encryption algorithms in early implementations of wireless (also known as Wi-Fi) were easily cracked.[14]

The end result was that practically any user with a laptop, a free software program available on a half dozen Web sites, and a car could hack into corporate, private, and even government networks.

This phenomenon, named war driving after its bigger brother war dialing, involved randomly driving through neighborhoods with a wireless-enabled laptop and a scanning program. Every time the user drives within receiving range of a wireless access point, the computer program registers its existence and attempts to capture its access key, which the user must have. More advanced applications of this principle require a global positioning system (GPS) interface and a GPS system.

The user attaches the GPS to the laptop and then drives around the city. As the computer works its magic, the program records not only the wireless network address and possible password, but also the GPS coordinates. Armed with this data file, the user now has a veritable city map containing all the wireless networks available. Then all the user has to do is drive to this location and log in. In fact, the equipment necessary for this technique is so portable that kids carrying laptops, GPSs, and antennae in their backpack could pull this off while walking around the city.

Another phenomenon that is seems to be more urban myth than reality is something called war chalking. Although I have located a number of web stories about the phenomenon, my research and physical searching has yet to uncover a single location. War chalking is derived from the old tradition used by hobos while traveling the rails of marking spots along the main line with symbols as guides for others to follow. For example, one particular symbol might signify that locals were receptive to hobos and frequently offered food or shelter.[15]

The war-driving community has allegedly adopted a similar symbol system for marking locations where users have found wireless access. These symbols are supposed to inform wireless hobos where access points are located, what the ID and password are, and whether encryption is enabled. For example, if a war driver finds an unsecured wireless network at a local Starbucks, she would mark the pavement, a wall, or a telephone pole nearby with a symbol revealing the wireless appearance point (AP) presence. This is supposed to save future wireless hobos from having war drive on their own.

I have yet to confirm, at least in south Florida, that war chalking is a widespread phenomenon. My guess that, instead, like many computer security issues, it is a mixture of hyperbole and truth.

Regardless of whether war chalking exists as a substantial phenomenon, it is a fact that wireless networks by nature are less secure than wired ones. As the wireless protocols have evolved (802.11g is the standard as of this writing), so too has the encryption standard attached to it. Although the wireless standard is not the most robust security measure in existence, the improved standards are moving in the right direction.

The biggest threat to wireless security is not the inherent vulnerability of the protocol but instead the vulnerability of the implementation. By default, most wireless appearance points are configured with passwords and authentication off. What this means is that most users, especially home users, can plug in the network interface and away they go. Leaving the appearance point in its default configuration means that no password authorization is required and this "open" network is available for access to anyone within receiving range. War drivers rely on user carelessness like this for easy and quick access to computer networks. One of the most powerful protections against network intrusions through wireless networks is simply enabling the built-in password protection.

One hidden vulnerability of wireless networks derives not from the underlying vulnerability of the encryption but from the tendency of computer users to expand the system beyond the administrator's original plan and without his or her knowledge. When authorized users introduce unauthorized components into a system, a vulnerability is created. For example, if an office has a relatively secure wireless LAN connecting the employees of a particular workgroup, the resources dedicated to the LAN are most likely under the control of a system administrator, who is responsible for adding and deleting nodes from the system. In a conventional wired topology, the addition of a node to the network requires reconfiguration of the physical parameters of the network—wires must be added or removed. In the wireless domain, there is no such need.

Say an employee who has a personal laptop that he also uses for company business decides that it would be more convenient to access the company internet on his laptop so that he can copy files from the server directly to his hard drive. In order to do this, assuming he has a wireless-enabled laptop, he simply needs to bring the laptop into the area of the appearance point. Depending on the configuration of the appearance point, it may or may not accept the log-in on that laptop. If it does, while the network itself is still secured and encryption protocols prevent outside intruders from accessing the net, the status of the employee's laptop is not so secure. The employee's computer may already be compromised by malware[16] or may be vulnerable to attack on its own; it might provide an outsider with a gateway into the office LAN. Thus, the dangers of wireless networks lurk in some hard-to-see places.[17]

No discussion of wireless network security would be complete without a brief mention of why wireless networks are compromised in the first place. Aside from the obvious reasons of stealing sensitive information, gaining top-secret data, or crashing a critical system, another more harmless reason exists—convenience. Today high-speed Internet connectivity is nearly standard in a majority of today's homes. What is less common is mobile Internet connectivity.

Although many major companies are now offering virtually worldwide Internet connectivity through cellular-style modems, they are not nearly as prevalent as the home/office-based Internet connectivity that has become part of our culture. While on the road, most computer users tend to go through withdrawal symptoms if they do not check their e-mail with regularity that would rival the most obsessive compulsive's regimen. What then do you do when no Internet connection is available? The answer is often simply to drive down any street in a local residential neighborhood until the laptop locates a signal. Log in, if it is unsecured, and hopscotch onto the Internet to download mail. Once you are done, close the laptop and drive away. Is this totally harmless behavior? There is no damage to the computer and no access to sensitive information.

A number of people see nothing wrong with this behavior, and even say that if the owner of the wireless network did not want people doing this, he or she could simply secure the network. Although this is true, the logic behind the justification hearkens back to the era of the original computer hackers and misperceives the nature of private versus public access. Even though no harm is done, ultimately the invading user has gained access to a private network, and as such, the behavior is highly suspect.

Another issue that arises is what I refer to as piggybacking. Very similar to the scenario in which someone surreptitiously taps into a neighbor's cable line, users in densely populated areas can easily piggyback onto the Internet using a nearby neighbor's unsecure wireless network. Although the wireless signal is not all that strong, it is usually strong enough to penetrate apartment walls and even across the road into a neighbor's house. If the network is unsecured, the neighbor will have access to that network connection and, assuming that the network is Internet enabled, to the owner's Internet account. Gaining access to Internet connectivity without paying for it is the modern equivalent of cable theft.

MALWARE

Even though computer hackers often gain the most media attention for their exploits, malware may have a greater potential for lasting damage. The term "malware" comes from *malicious software*. Often used to describe any number of potentially damaging forms of computer codes, the malware programs most often thought of are viruses, Trojan horses, and worms. More recently, however, adware and spyware have become part of the malware environment.

A computer *virus* is, at its heart, a self-perpetuating computer program that executes some code or portion of code without the knowledge and permission of the end user. Some viruses are harmless and exist only as a "proof of concept," while others exists for the sole purpose of wreaking havoc on unsuspecting users. While the term "virus" is often used interchangeably to all forms of computer malware, viruses, Trojan horse programs, and worms are slightly different programs.[18]

A virus is a computer program that has the innate ability to reproduce. This ability to reproduce, like a real virus, and copy themselves into other uninfected systems has made computer viruses particularly troublesome over the years. The malicious code that viruses carry can range from nuisance activity, to file destruction, to total system destruction.

Many viruses, in order to infect and affect as many computers as possible, will remain dormant for a particular length of time while continuing to replicate. Then, when a particular trigger event occurs, such as a date in the case of a time bomb, the dormant virus releases its payload and carries out its intended mission. If the trigger is a particular event, such as when the user clicks a particular icon, it is known as a logic bomb since the release of the payload is triggered by the logic of the computer program.

In the early days of computer viruses, the only method of distribution was on removable media, such as floppy disks. Computer bulletin boards and lately the Internet have changed that. As use of bulletin boards and the Internet to download programs and files grew, so did the prevalence of computer viruses. Today, computer viruses have a tremendously powerful distribution channel and can gain access to the entire Internet community nearly instantaneously.

Capitalizing on speed of the Internet, *worms* search out acceptable host systems and then copy themselves onto those systems. Hidden within the logic of the program itself is an algorithm that intelligently searches for computers on the network or Internet that are not yet infected. If the computers possess the appropriate environment, such as the proper version of an operating system or a particular web browser, the worms then copy themselves from the host computer onto the target computer. The Morris worm was one of the most successful and damaging computer worms.[19]

Written by Robert Tappan Morris, a Cornell University computer student, the Morris worm was created not with overt malicious intent but more as an attempt to see if it would work. The problem was that a programming error caused the worm to replicate at an excessive rate. The result of this little "academic experiment" was a nearly complete disruption of service to 10 percent of the all the computers attached to the Internet at the time. Additionally, Morris's little prank earned him a conviction under the 1986 Computer Fraud and Abuse Act; nevertheless, currently he is an associate professor at MIT.[20]

A *Trojan horse* program is named from the ancient story of the conquest of Troy. Like the original Trojan horse, from which the Greeks could not attack until the Trojans brought the horse into the city, Trojan horse programs cannot self-replicate, but instead require the user to take some action.[21] For example, photographic images and e-mails are common carriers of Trojan horse programs. Just as Odysseus and his soldiers emerged from the Trojan horse on the unsuspecting city of Troy while its soldiers slumbered, once the user downloads the e-mail or graphic file in which the malicious code is hidden, the Trojan program will begin destroying computer data (if that is what its mission is).

It is sometimes easier to think of a Trojan horse as a delivery method rather than a piece of malicious code itself. The fact that there must be some user interaction, such as downloading and opening an e-mail or a graphics file, makes Trojans what they are. The reality is that their payload can be nearly anything—a virus, a computer worm, or in most recent cases, adware and spyware.

Trojan horses are common methods of deploying packet sniffers, password collectors, or backdoors. Packet sniffers are small computer programs that sit on a network and monitor all traffic that flows on the network. Depending on their design, packet sniffers may be written to collect sensitive data, such as user names and passwords, or e-mail traffic in the case of corporate espionage.[22] Backdoors are programs that create a hidden entry point to a system. This backdoor allows computer hackers to surreptitiously log into the computer system undetected.[23]

As the power of web browsers such as Internet Explorer has increased, the ability of hackers to deploy Trojan horses has grown as well. One method of deployment is through Web sites that make use of advanced features such as ActiveX and Java to conceal snippets of malicious code on web pages. These code snippets are adept at exploiting known bugs in the web browser or operating system, and then "trick" the system into running the malicious code as though it were a legitimate process. Some of the most virulent Trojan programs recently have been very good at exploiting bugs in the Windows operating system.

As mentioned, another common method of Trojan deployment is through e-mail. Trojan horse programs can piggyback on legitimate-looking e-mails. Unsuspecting users launch these programs, which are identified as urgent messages and masquerade as a text file. The program may make it appear that the file is doing what it purports to do, such as opening a text file, but in reality it is carrying out its clandestine mission in the background. Again, depending on the nature of the payload program, this could be anything from copying files to collecting password information.

Adware and spyware are two more recent forms of malicious computer programming. While adware, in its original form is not particularly malicious, it is annoying. *Adware* is designed to present users with banner advertising and pop-ups that trumpet new programs, Web sites, and software. These types of programs are often part of an advertising campaign; although annoying to the end user, they are not particularly dangerous to the computer. Spyware is more heinous.

Spyware is a computer program or code script that covertly monitors a computer user's activity. The spyware program then forwards that information to whoever deployed it in the first place. Allegedly used primarily as a way of gauging buyer preferences and user demographics, spyware often collects data about buying patterns and Web site traffic trends. Use of spyware is quite popular among pornographic providers.

Although the "legitimate" use of spyware, while questionable, is not particularly malicious, the more unsavory uses raise issues of concern. Like the methodology employed by Trojan horse programs, spyware programs can be used for any number of unscrupulous tasks, such as collecting password information, keystroke monitoring, and activity tracking. All of these activities might be legitimate activities in certain circumstances, such as a corporate environment or secure government facility, but their use against unsuspecting Internet travelers is highly unethical.

No discussion of modern malware would be complete without at least a brief discussion of rootkits.

A *rootkit* is a set of computer tools that is designed to create a backdoor into a computer system and then conceal itself from view. While the concept is not new, the implementation used by modern rootkits has made them of particularly high concern to computer security professionals.[24]

Most often, hackers deploy a rootkit on a system in order to give themselves backdoor access to an otherwise secure system. This is not a new practice. As computer security administrators become more and more vigilant, frequent polling of the system reveals unauthorized processes running and leads to the discovery of the intruder. The key to identifying an intruder is examining the computer system's own process data. After all, who better to know exactly what is going on than the computer itself? This process can be very successful since the system administrator is polling the information at the system level.

Hackers realize this vulnerability exists, and they have responded with the powerful hooking device that allows the rootkit to highjack the system processes polled by the system administrator and report back whatever the hackers desire. For example, the system administrator will query the system regarding running processes, logged in users, and open ports. The information that is returned is whatever the hacker has programmed the rootkit to reply with.[25]

Some of these implementations are very difficult to detect using conventional virus protection software, which often relies on reports of processes from the operating system system level. By hooking the program code that is called by the virus protection software, the rootkit can report back false information that effectively makes its existence invisible to the virus protection software. Likewise, depending on how the actual rootkit is implemented, no system data reported by the operating system can be considered accurate. In the proper hands, rootkits can offer hackers nearly total system access.

ATTACKS FROM THE INSIDE

In the last section, we talked about the threat to computer systems from outside attackers. While this type of attack often gets the most media attention, it is not the only threat to a computer installation. Computer installations also face a significant risk of compromise due to employee misconduct. Here we look at the various ways in which insiders can negatively impact a computer installation and what types of scenarios computer forensic investigators are likely to encounter.

One threat to information security lies in the employee acting as a spy for the competition. In today's highly competitive corporate world, corporate Web sites, advertising campaigns, and intellectual property holdings are all valuable tools in the race to dominate market share. In this information-is-king world, the one who holds the information succeeds in the market. Whether the information is market data, more efficient processing, or original inventions, every business takes extraordinary steps to safeguard it.

Take for example, the "secret" Coca-Cola formula. The value of the formula in terms of competitive advantage is high only so long as the formula does in fact stay secret. The moment that the secret is out, anyone can replicate the taste that for so long has been the flagship product upon which an empire has been built.

Recent arrests confirm the seriousness with which corporations guard their secrets. In early 2006 three people were arrested and charged federally, with attempting to sell secrets of the Coca-Cola corporation to executives at Pepsi.[26] One of the alleged conspirators, an administrative assistant for a Coca-Cola executive, is accused of taking trade secret information from corporate files and stuffing a new Coke product into a handbag, and attempting to sell them to Coca-Cola's competitors.

Although few businesses have secrets as valuable as the formula for the Coca-Cola soft drink, many have trade secrets and information that is valuable to them. In some cases, the drive to overcome a competitor's market advantage may provide the incentive to engage in spying. Corporate spying, also known as corporate espionage, involves using any means at your disposal, both legal and illegal, to gather enough information from your competitors to overtake them in the market race. This information warfare is nothing new.

In fact, market competitors have been engaging in tactics like dumpster diving and workforce infiltration for a number of years. The difference that the information age has brought is the efficiency with which businesses can sift through competitors' garbage.

Spyware and keystroke loggers are powerful tools for passing along information about the internal business of a competitor. Even when insider help is not available, keystroke monitors can send back every bit of information that traverses a competitor's intranet—including passwords and highly sensitive trade secret data.

An additional inside threat is the disgruntled employee. Disgruntled employees can pose a real threat to the company through sabotage and digital ransom. Sabotage can come in many forms, from destruction of physical assets of the company, to theft of trade secrets. Either way, the assets involved are likely to be valuable to the company, and their loss could seriously impact its future solvency.

File ransom is a combination of revenge and profiteering. Ransoming can occur in a number of ways, but the most obvious involves cryptography. In this scenario, the disgruntled employee captures vital data and then encrypts it using a high-level encryption algorithm. Then he encrypts the key, erases the vital data using a wiping program to ensure that all traces of the information are gone, and sends the ransom demand and the encrypted key to the company.

If the company pays the ransom, the disgruntled employee simply e-mails the key to the encrypted key, allowing the company to unencrypt the key and unencrypt the data. A similar scenario was reported in late 2005 by the software security company Symantec. In that scenario, known vulnerabilities of the Windows Internet Explorer were exploited to download a Trojan horse program known as Trojan.Pgpcoder.A onto computers of visitors to some compromised Web sites. The Trojan program proceeded to encrypt document and text files and generate an e-mail demanding payment of money in return for the keys to the files.[27] This scheme is not widespread, and in the case reported by Symantec, experts used digital cryptanalysis techniques (code breaking) to decode the files and avoid paying the ransom; however, as the attack method becomes more refined and begins using more robust encryption techniques, it could prove to be a very annoying trend.

E-mail wiretaps are not limited to the FBI's Carnivore software. Instead, installing illegal wiretaps may be as simple as encoding a small piece of Java script in the HTML body of an e-mail message. This code sends copies of the e-mail back to the sender every time the e-mail is forwarded. For example, if an employee wants to gather information from the company, she could encode the wiretap script into an e-mail and send it to coworkers, requesting that each recipient forward it to someone else in the company. Every time the e-mail is forwarded, a copy goes to the address in the script. If the content of the e-mails is sensitive, that information is carried along with it. Because many people simply hit "reply," illegal e-mail wiretaps could be fairly easy to pull off.[28]

However, the way this wiretap is executed makes it unlikely to be highly successful in a company with a robust information technology (IT) security policy. Several factors limit the Trojan's power. First, in order to work, the program requires the user to run Java-enabled e-mail reading software. All the major readers, such as Outlook and Eudora, are Java enabled, but this feature can be disabled. A strong IT security policy will ensure that the default for these readers is set to disable Java. This will prevent the remailing action on that particular machine, but the next recipient who receives the e-mail who is running Java-enabled software will send the data to the initiator. As you can see, the IT security plan is only as strong as its weakest link.

Another less high-tech problem with the e-mail wiretap scenario is that extra messages will appear in the recipient's "outbox." Although careless users may not think anything of this, vigilant employees will notice that their accounts are sending more e-mail messages than they actually dispatched. That, combined with the fact that the originating e-mail address will lead investigators directly to the originator, makes this a less-than-ideal method of eavesdropping on coworkers.

Given the weaknesses of this method of corporate attack, this represents a fairly low threat to corporate information security. Nonetheless, IT security policies must address the threat, because no matter how simple the attack may be, it can be effective to the unprepared.

In previous sections I have discussed the threat of outside intruders gaining unauthorized access to computer resources. Even though this is the scenario most people think of, a more likely threat is unauthorized access by insiders. Employees with computer expertise already have access to the system. In most systems, depending on the operating system in use, user access is granted based on permissions. Each level of permissions allows that user to do only those things that are part of her permission group. Read-level permissions allow users only to read files; read/write permissions allow users to read and write to files; and so on. The most powerful of these permissions will allow users to execute programs.

In addition to the file permission level controls in most operating systems, administrators can restrict user access to certain resources and certain parts of the file system. For example, users may be given read/write access to the company filer server but no access at all to the drive or partition on which the operating system is stored. This added level of protection, combined with restriction on the ability to execute code, shields the system from malicious scripts and rootkits installed by authorized users.

In most well-designed secure systems, root-level access (the most powerful level of access) is restricted to the top system administrator or at most a very small number of highly trusted employees. In truth, most employees need nothing more than basic read/write access to the data files.

Like the outsider who is seeking to gain control over a company's IT resources, disgruntled employees or spies are looking to promote their access level. Insiders have the added benefit of already having access to the system. All the techniques available to computer hackers on the outside are available to inside hackers. By locating weaknesses in the operating system and installing code to exploit these weaknesses, insiders could promote their access level to that of superuser.[29] Once they have gained this level of permissions on their account, it is a trivial matter to create a new account or backdoor, covering their tracks, and restoring their original account to its original user access level.

A highly skilled hacker can infiltrate the system from the inside and remain hidden in the user accounts for as long as he needs to collect the information necessary to pass along to competitors. By utilizing dormant accounts and phantom employees, computer hackers assume the identities of legitimate users, remaining transparent to all but the most vigilant system administrators. To make matters worse, an inexperienced system administrator may be more focused on threats from the outside than from the inside and inadvertently overlook the telltale signs of authorized user account abuse.

It is important to discuss briefly what information may be of particular interest to inside hackers. For starters, these include the very computing resources of the target company. In large companies with mainframe computers, the computing resources can be tremendous. Cray supercomputers and IBM mainframes often have the processing power of thousands of desktop computers. Access to such a processing behemoth could allow hackers to utilize the computing resources to run clandestine programs that require a lot of computer clock cycles.

One example of just such a situation would be where password cracking or cryptanalysis is necessary. Password cracking using brute-force or dictionary attacks requires tremendous amounts of computer processing power to be efficient. Likewise, cryptanalysis on breakable yet strong algorithms can require hundreds of thousands or even hundreds of millions of clock cycles in order to break the key. This level of power is not available to the average desktop user. Hackers solve this problem by gaining clandestine access to a supercomputer and running the code-breaking programs on the mainframe.

Another target for hackers could be information. As discussed earlier, information is power. In the competitive business world, information often takes the form of customer databases, computer algorithms, and patents. Often tremendous amounts of company resources are devoted to the research and development of patents and trade secrets. The goal of hackers in this case would be to pirate the data and profit by selling it to the competition.

One final and often overlooked reason for an insider to promote access to company resources is for personal gain—employees may be moonlighting. For example, computer programmers and IT personnel have been known to run side businesses. Access to powerful computer resources and computer software could give them a competitive advantage. This moonlighting situation becomes even more troublesome when the employee either directly or indirectly competes with the employer company. From an employee loyalty perspective, this is an undesirable situation, but from the IT security perspective, it is even more problematic.

Employees use company resources for private profit in many different ways. When computer users who have limited access to corporate IT resources promote their user privileges, it creates not only ethical issues but can also result in compromised data security and overall reduced system security.

Along the same lines are concerns over employee theft. As I said earlier, employee theft of company resources occurs in all facets of the business world. Whether it is pilfered staples and envelopes or personal copies on the company machine, the problem results in lowered revenues.

However, when employee theft includes computer software, the potential for loss can be tremendous. With the cost of updating and upgrading software spiraling ever upward, employees have growing incentives to "copy" company software onto personal computers. While policies in most companies address this problem, not all are equally quick to police it.

When the price for a single-user license of popular word processing and spreadsheet programs runs into the hundreds of dollars, it is fairly easy for employees to justify what they perceive as harmless copying. After all, they might rationalize, there is no real harm done, the computer companies make millions anyway, what's one harmless copy. While the rationalization may ring more or less true for some, the bottom line is that the copying is in fact a violation of the licensing agreement between the software developer and the company—as well as probably being illegal under several different federal laws.

When companies fail to take appropriate precautions by limiting access to computer software and controlling who and when such software is loaded onto computers, they open themselves up to employee pilferage. On the same note, control of who can load software onto company computers is also a concern.

Many companies believe that they can increase employee productivity by issuing laptops. Between Wi-Fi connectivity and 24/7 access to company data, the cost of hardware and software is easily justified in most cases. The underlying problems, however, may not come to light until much later on. As I illustrated in the section on wireless connectivity, employee behavior can leave company networks unnecessarily vulnerable—sometimes without IT staff even being aware of it. This problem can be magnified when employees have the ability to install software on their company-issued laptops.

Although system administrators can control access to administrative rights to install hardware and software, often they do not do so. Whether because the administrators are too lazy to adjust each and every laptop, or simply because they want to make life easier for employees, some administrators grant administrative-level access to employees. This allows users to modify and tweak their laptops to suit their own particular working style. It also allows them to install programs. Some of these programs may originate in questionable sources or may be illegal copies.

Software from questionable sources can carry viruses, worms, or Trojan horse programs that may eventually disable the entire company network. Likewise, software from questionable sources may not "play nice" with the software already installed on the company's servers. In this case, the malicious activity of the third-party software, while unintentional, is no less damaging, requiring system administrators to repair damaged data and, in extreme cases, reformat entire terabyte-sized hard drives. The result is down-time, overtime, and an all-around bad time for the IT staff.

To avoid these nightmare scenarios, system administrators should carefully monitor the access levels that their users have and should make sure the any software approved for installation is both legitimate and safe. Doing so will greatly increase the likelihood of a smoothly functioning installation.

As a final topic, I must mention a problem that is not inherently digital, but very much a problem nonetheless—theft. Employees in all areas of the business may have the opportunity to remove company assets. Computer assets are no different. Much like the pilferage of paper clips I mentioned earlier, employee theft of company digital resources can range from the somewhat negligible to the downright debilitating. Tossing a few blank CD-Rs into the briefcase, while easily justified by most employees, should be viewed no differently from removing a 150-gigabyte hard drive from the company computer and walking out the door with it. The only difference is the value of the individual item; theft, however, is still theft. Companies that maintain an inventory of digital resources need to ensure that their policies are designed to protect from loss and that their IT staff are trained to enforce the policy.

CONCLUSION

In this chapter, I have focused on some of the more prevalent threats to computer systems from both the outside and the inside. We have looked at the traditional hacker community and some of its variations. We have also taken a glimpse at what the future may hold in terms of computer warfare. Cyberterrorism has yet to rain down the sort of destruction that terrorist acts such as the 9/11 bombings have done. That does not mean that cyberterror is not a very real threat. In fact, the power of the bit and byte could well be a hundred times more powerful than the airliners that struck the World Trade Towers.

I have given you a brief look at some of the most common forms of software that are used to attack computers. While malware attacks from the inside, they are normally deployed by unwelcome intruders from outside the computer network. Like these outsiders, individuals inside the organization also have the power to create untold levels of damage to a computer system.

However, unlike outside intruders, insiders often have much greater access to computer resources. The familiarity and trust that most computer administrators have with computer users under their control is often the most vulnerable point for a computer system. Recognizing this fact of life can help computer administrators guard against the enemy within and reduce the amount of loss attributable to trusted source attacks.

In the next chapter, I begin discussing some of the ways in which criminals use computers to further their criminal design. Whether their crime is a conventional one, such as theft, or a digital one, such as music piracy, criminals have learned to harness the power of the computer to enhance their criminal repertoire and gain a competitive advantage.

NOTES

1. See generally Steven Levy, *Hackers: Heroes of the Computer Revolution* (New York: Penguin Books, 1994).

2. See generally Douglas Thomas, *Hacker Culture* (Minneapolis: University of Minnesota Press, 2002), pp. 56–61, discussing hacking language games.

3. Bernadette H. Schell and John L. Dodge, *The Hacking of America: Who's Doing It, Why, and How* (Westport, CT: Quorum Books, 2002), pp. 64–65.

4. Ibid., pp. 29–33.

5. Schell and Dodge, *The Hacking of America,* pp. 4, 56–70.

6. Ibid., pp. 44–48, 50.

7. Robert Moore, *Cybercrime: Investigating High-Technology Computer Crime* (Cincinnati, OH: Anderson Publishing), pp. 24–25.

8. Schell and Dodge, *The Hacking of America*, pp. 76–77.

9. See generally Thomas, *Hacker Culture*.

10. Moore, *Cybercrime*, p. 25. See also generally Schell and Dodge, *The Hacking of America*.

11. Ibid., p. 26.

12. Bernaette H. Schell and Clemens Martin, *Cybercrime: A Reference Handbook* (Santa Barbara, CA: ABC-Clio, 2004), p. 11.

13. IEEE 802.11, also known as Wi-Fi, is a standard protocol for wireless communications that was developed by the IEEE committee on network communications in order to standardize wireless communications devices and how they talk to one another.

14. Eoghan Casey, *Digital Evidence and Computer Crime: Forensic Science, Computers and the Internet* (Boston, MA: Elsevier Academic Press, 2004), pp. 367–368.

15. Ben Hammersly, "Working the Web: Warchalking," Guardian Unlimited, July 4, 2002, http://technology.guardian.co.uk/online/story/0,3605,748499,00.html.

16. Malware is a term that is often used to describe any software installed on a computer that causes harm. For example, virus, adware, spyware, and Trojan horse programs are all types of malware.

17. John Vacca, *Computer Forensics: Computer Crime Scene Investigation* (Hingham, MA: Charles River Media, 2002), pp. 502–503.

18. Schell and Martin, *Cybercrime*. pp. 60–62.

19. Ibid., pp. 3–4.

20. Ibid.

21. Moore, *Cybercrime,* pp. 36–37.

22. Vacca, *Computer Forensics,* p. 448.

23. Schell and Martin, *Cybercrime,* p. 67.

24. Christopher L. T. Brown, *Computer Evidence: Collection & Preservation* (Hingham, MA: Charles River Media, 2006), pp. 115–120.

25. Ibid.

26. Associated Press. 2006. Pepsi Alerted Coca-Cola to Stolen Coke Secrets Offer, July 6, 2006. http://www.foxnews.com/story/0,2933, 202439,00.html.

27. Alexandra Gamanenko, " 'Ransom Trojan' Uses Cryptography for Malicious Purposes," Ezine Articles, http://ezinearticles.com/?Ransom-Trojan-Uses-Cryptography-for-Malicious-Purpose&id=39179.

28. Jay Lyman, "Microsoft E-Mail 'Out of Control,' " *Newsfactor Magazine* Online, February 2, 2001,www.newsfactor.com/perl/story/ 7229.html. See also Thomas C. Greene, "JavaScript Makes E-Mail Bugging Easy," *The Register,* February 7, 2001, available at: www.theregister.co.uk/2001/02/07/javascript_makes_email_bugging_ easy/; Matthew Broersma, "E-mail 'Wiretap' Could Expose Your Messages to Prying Eyes," ZDNet News, February 4, 2001, available at: http://news.zdnet.com/2100–9595_22-527914.html.

29. The term "superuser" originated in the world of UNIX hacking, but it has expanded into other systems as well. A superuser is someone who has unlimited access to files. This is also the functional equivalent of root access or administrator access. See generally Eric S. Raymond, ed., *The New Hacker's Dictionary* (Cambridge, MA: MIT Press, 1991).

SUGGESTED READING

Levy, Steven. *Crypto: How the Code Rebels Beat the Government—Saving Privacy in the Digital Age.* New York: Viking Press, 2001.

Schell, Bernadette H., and John L. Dodge, *The Hacking of America: Who's Doing It, Why and How.* Westport, CT: Quoroum Books, 2002.

Schell, Bernadette H., and Clemens Martin. *Cybercrime: A Reference Handbook.* Santa Barbara, CA: ABC-CLIO, 2004.

Thomas, Douglas. *Hacker Culture.* Minneapolis: University of Minnesota Press, 2002.

7

COMPUTERS AS TOOLS FOR EVIL

INTRODUCTION

In this chapter, we look at the way in which criminals employ computers to further their illegal activity. Traditionally, the topic of computer crime has been segregated into those crimes that are strictly computer in nature, such as computer trespasses and theft of computer data. Lately, the more reasonable view is that any crime in which a computer is used in some aspect of the offense can be considered a computer crime. Although this definition is sweeping and could lead to overinclusion, it is a good starting point for discussing computers as they relate to criminal activity.

COMPUTERS AND CRIME

As I mentioned, in the early days of computers, computer crime was that narrowly defined area of criminal conduct involving thefts from computers or attacks on computers. The quintessential hacker cases that were first prosecuted involved just such incidents. As computer use has grown, and the power computers give their owners has grown, criminals have quickly capitalized on this power to make their nondigital crimes more efficient.

For example, narcotics dealers and bookmakers now keep their records in computer databases secured by strong encryption. Forgers and counterfeiters use high-quality laser printers, scanners, and imaging software to create phony documents nearly indistinguishable from the originals, and even street-level criminals have been known to use personal data assistants (PDAs) and digital address books to maintain customer records and "owe sheets" in order to run a more organized business. Computer technology has infiltrated every level of the criminal organization.

For this reason, the need for police and investigators to be computer literate at the very least and computer proficient at best continues to grow. Police officer and investigators can no longer avoid embracing the technology that their competition has turned to. One step in the right direction means understanding how criminals have harnessed computer power in different areas.

IDENTITY THEFT

Identity theft is probably the most often discussed form of computer-assisted crime today. Whether you are reading the newspaper, watching the six o'clock news, or surfing the Internet, chances are very good you will run across a story about identity theft and the dangers to consumers.

The dangers of identify theft are real. Identity thieves are responsible for millions of dollars in losses by consumers each year, and true to prediction, their attacks have become more sophisticated and losses continue to climb each year. The Federal Trade Commission (FTC) acts as a clearinghouse for identity theft complaints. According to the FTC's most recent statistics, nearly 700,000 fraud complaints were lodged with its Sentinel Web site in 2005. Thirty-seven percent of these complaints were for identity theft. This equates to nearly 256,000 complaints—an increase of nearly 20 percent over 2003.[1]

At its most basic, identity theft involves a criminal assuming the identity of a victim in order to get credit and buy merchandise with no intention of repaying the debt. Thieves carry out this scheme in many ways, not all of which are digital.

Dumpster diving is a tried and true method employed by identity thieves that predates computer schemes by a dozen or so years. Dumpster diving is exactly what it sounds like. Thieves, armed with rubber gloves, a garbage bag filled with soda cans, and a flashlight, begin climbing into garbage dumpsters. The garbage bag and soda cans are not essential to the mission but give divers a plausible excuse when confronted—they are merely searching for cans to recycle.

The divers rummage through garbage and discarded papers looking for bits and pieces of a victim's information. Bank statements, credit card receipts, utility bills, and preapproved offers of credit are very valuable finds for the identity thief. In fact, almost anything that contains even the tiniest bit of personal information can add a piece to the identity puzzle that the thieves are trying to assemble.[2]

Once they have collected enough bits and pieces of who you are, they have all the information necessary to assume your identity. Then, armed with your personal information, they can move on to the next step in the process.

Dumpster diving is not the only way that thieves can get your information. For example, shoulder surfing and card skimming are popular too. Shoulder surfing is an age-old method of stealing personal information—in this case credit card numbers. The surfer stands in line behind the target. When the target presents her credit card for payment, the surfer, peering over the victim's shoulder, memorizes the 16-digit credit card number. Card skimming is a similar principle except it relies more on technology and a trusted accomplice.

In a card skimming operation, the thief or an accomplice gains employment in a retail establishment. In this job, the thief is in a great position to come into contact with many credit cards daily. Then, using a skimming device (a credit card reader that does nothing more than record the numbers to a file), the thief collects hundreds or even thousands of credit card numbers each day.

The skimmer may swipe the card twice, once in the clandestine reader to collect the data from the card and the second time to actually process the transaction through the retail point of sale (POS) terminal. Computer-savvy hackers may be able to dispense with the skimming device if they are skilled enough to hack the POS terminal and copy the credit card information to a disk.[3]

Variations on this theme abound and are limited only by the thieves' ingenuity. One variation involves two or more accomplices and an unwitting store clerk. This scam combines a bit of social engineering with the shoulder surfing scheme. It is most successful when attempted during busy retail times, such as the period between Thanksgiving and Christmas. The surfer targets a potential victim in a busy retail store. The surfer gets in line in such a way as to be partially obscured from the clerk's view. When the mark reaches the checkout and offers either a credit card or check for authorization as payment, the surfer's accomplice telephones the unwitting clerk posing as security for either a credit card company or bank. Then the highly skilled social engineer convinces the clerk that the target is suspected in a forgery or a fraud scheme and he needs to confirm the information. Skilled callers can convince the clerk to read back the credit card number or check number over the telephone; then the caller or the in-store accomplice records the number. The caller then informs the clerk that the target was not the person being sought, and the target leaves the store none the wiser.

A number of schemes involving employees of various companies exist. In these "trusted entity scams," employees provide identity thieves with listings of credit card numbers or customers' personal data in return for finders' fees. Clerks and managers with access to daily transaction records can provide a nearly endless supply of information to fraudsters. The fraudsters then simply generate forged credit cards and run up exorbitant bills with no intention of repaying them.[4]

The identity theft scheme is only complete once fraudsters have been successful in purchasing merchandise on the credit of another person's account. To do this, thieves employ a number of different techniques. One of the most difficult to pull off is the actual forgery of a credit card.

The technology for making a credit card is fairly simple. All thieves need are the proper numbers, which they have gotten through one of the above means, a few credit card blanks, which can be purchased in bulk from a number of Internet sources (for example, www.cpicardgroup.com/index.htm), and a magnetic stripe encoder. The encoder, the most sophisticated part of the equation, is a simple computer peripheral that writes the account information on the magnetic stripe on the back of the card. These also are available from a number of Internet sources (for example, www.positivelypos.com/id_tech_magnetic_card_encoder.html/).

Armed with a list of account numbers, blanks, and the encoder, thieves can create a few hundred "credit cards" in the space of a few hours. The encoding process is the easy part of the process. The difficult part is duplicating the look of the credit card itself. Most banks and issuing companies have enhanced the security features on their credit cards to a level that rivals the features used by the U.S. Treasury to protect currency. Microprinting, holder photos, holographic images, and security codes are all highly successful and difficult-to-defeat security features that make credit card forgery a high-cost, low-return investment. In short, forged credit cards are difficult to pass reliably, and the effort required often makes them unattractive to individual fraudsters. Large groups of organized criminals, however, can operate on the principle of economies of scale; with a large initial investment, they can produce thousands of high-quality cards. In the long run, their return on investment is high because of the sheer volume of cards they can generate.[5]

The alternatives for the small identity thief are more limited. One such alternative again involves an accomplice in retail. In this scam, the identity thief provides the retail accomplice with the "credit cards"—nothing more than plain white card blanks with the encoded information on them. The accomplice runs a number of transactions through the register by swiping the fake cards and pocketing the same amount of money. The register balances, until the card company declines the fraudulent charges. This scheme, while short-lived, can be lucrative.

Another more long-term alternative is mail order. Armed with a credit or debit card and an Internet connection, nearly anything your heart desires is literally at your fingertips. Web retailers such as Amazon and Overstock, not to mention traditional brick-and-mortar businesses that have extended their business to online sales, offer nearly every possible consumer product by mail. Most of these "stores" readily accept credit cards. Fraudsters armed with enough personal information and a credit card can place orders using stolen credit cards.

With the rise in popularity of this type of retail transaction, businesses have begun instituting procedural safeguards such as requiring verification numbers, address matching, and in some cases, requiring direct customer confirmation. Notwithstanding these increased security measures, identity thieves continue to have a fair amount of success in pulling off these schemes.

One reason for such continued success is that identity theft is often discovered only months after the crime. By that time, the thief is long gone, and the trail leading to him is cold. Consumers who do not carefully scrutinize their bank statements and credit card bills are likely to miss small charges to online retailers until long after they have been victimized. Additionally, large-scale identity theft involving more than mere credit cards can remain undiscovered by a lax consumer until months later.[6]

Not all identity theft scenarios involve the theft of credit card information. Some are more ambitious than that, involving real estate, mortgages, and automobiles. In reality, the identity fraud scheme can involve nearly any type of property upon which some sort of security interest can be granted. Schemes of this nature can result in loses to consumers and creditor in the range of hundreds of thousand of dollars.

Perhaps the most talked about form of identity theft is the fairly recent phenomenon involving the Internet known as phishing. This Johnny-come-lately to identity theft is really nothing more than a new, techno-savvy way in which identity thieves steal your personal information. As I mentioned, identity theft was around long before the Internet became popular. However, like most things, the Internet and digital technology have made identity theft more efficient.

Phishing is a combination of social engineering and computer hacking. It is social engineering because it plays on human nature in order to trick us into providing private information. It is computer hacking because in the beginning, it capitalized on a bug in the Microsoft Internet Explorer web browser that made it possible to conceal a Web site's true identity from the user. By combining these two techniques, identity thieves have conned thousands of people into divulging sensitive information.[7]

Phishing most often begins when targets receive an official-looking e-mail warning them of some impending problem if they do not act now. For example, a common approach is to warn targets that their account at the local bank is believed to have been compromised. Targets are then warned that unless they log into their account to verify their information, they may be responsible for all the fraudulent charges levied against their account. The e-mail, which seems very professional and helpful, even presents users with a hyperlink to the bank's Web site, making rectifying the situation as simple as clicking the mouse.

The rub in this case is that the hyperlink directs users not to the bank's legitimate Web site but instead to a phony site created by the fraudsters. This is where the computer hacker part comes in. Earlier versions of Internet Explorer contained a bug that would cause the status bar to drop all the characters after a particular sequence of control characters. Capitalizing on this, fraudsters create a web address using the root of the legitimate site, such as www.targetsbank.com, and then append to that uniform resource locator (URL) information directing the browser to their fake site. The programming bug fools the browser into displaying only the address for the legitimate site, tricking users into believing they are really on their bank's Web site.[8]

To make matters worse, identity thieves go to great lengths to make their fake site look exactly like the legitimate site, even going as far as copying logos and graphics. Once unsuspecting users land on the fake site, they are asked to input their username and password, just as they would on their real bank's Web site. The rest is elementary for the fraudsters.

Armed with the targets' username and password, fraudsters now have access to all of the targets' banking information and can order any sort of transfers and transaction the bank's Web site offers. Identity thieves can carry the scheme further by requiring targets to verify other key pieces of information, such as date of birth, social security number, and driver's license number. Armed with this new information, the thieves have access not only to victims' bank accounts but also to all the personal information necessary to apply for numerous credit cards.

Last, on the topic of identity theft, you cannot overlook the possibility that sensitive information may be compromised by the very people entrusted with securing it. Credit card companies, government agencies, and businesses have all been accused of playing fast and loose with consumer information from time to time. In fact, the recent highly publicized compromise of thousands of veterans' personal information illustrates this fact quite well.[9]

Sometimes the compromise may be accidental, and other times it may be part of a larger, more heinous plan. Employees of information clearinghouses have thousands and thousands of bytes of personal data under their control. Unauthorized copying and dissemination can lead to nearly epidemic levels of identity theft. In some situations, employees may become compromised after they are hired; others seek employment or promotion so that they can pass information along to outside accomplices. Either way, release of personal data opens the door for identity theft and all its attendant ramifications.

Perhaps the most talked about problem recently, identity theft is hardly the only crime that computer technology has had an impact on. One other such crime is child endangerment.

In the traditional world, child endangerment has been a problem for as long as recorded history. Victimization of children seems to mobilize a core fear in the community like no other crime, even murder. With the growth of computers and the Internet in particular, child victimization has developed a new face: the Internet predator.

Internet predation, much like many other forms of computer crime, is at its heart a traditional crime with an added digital twist. In order to better understand the twist that computers give to child endangerment, we must look at it in the two spheres that I became familiar with in my nearly two decades in law enforcement pursuing predators: child pornography and online solicitation.

Child pornography, like adult pornography, has probably existed for as long as humans have been able to draw figures on cave walls. The Internet, however, has added the new dimension of mobility. Child pornographers are at their heart collectors. Much like philatelists or numismatists, they endeavor to add to their collection and watch it grow. Also like other collectors, child pornographers tend to gravitate toward others who share their "hobby."

Before the Internet, child pornographers still collected images. Instead of downloading them, they mail-ordered them from foreign countries and met fellow collectors on Far East junkets designed to provide an outlet for behavior that society has universally condemned. Despite the difficulties inherent with seeking out others with similar illegal dispositions, child pornographers managed to locate others with whom they could exchange trophies and stories.

Likewise, pre-Internet child pornographers successfully targeted and recruited children to infuse new images into their growing collection of prized specimens. The difference between pre-Internet child pornography and today's landscape is not so much that there is more of it; it is that access and networking are much more efficient.

In the world before the Internet a child pornographer had to risk a great deal to identify, target, and solicit a child. In the Internet world of near-total anonymity, pornographers are free to hide behind whatever pseudonym they choose and reach out across limitless miles looking for a victim. Not only can they do this anonymously, they can do it efficiently and without borders.

Traditional child pornographers were forced to search local schoolyards, malls, and playgrounds for new targets. This reality made their search dangerous and the potential for exposure great. Now that the Internet has come along, chat rooms, e-mail, and blogs have replaced the search on the playground and in the mall. Child predators posing as interested, caring peers no longer need to offer the hopes of petting a stray puppy, when they can simply engage children in peer-to-peer banter.

Associating with fellow predators and sharing experiences and images has become much easier. At the click of a mouse button, hundreds of illegal images can hurtle across hundreds of miles of ether-space to waiting predators in different time zones. This efficiency, combined with the fact that most parents who would have never considered sending their young child to the corner playground unsupervised, allow that same child unfettered access to the household computer and its Internet connection, make the Internet fertile ground for child predators.

Along with the specter of immediate access to victims, computer technology brings another aspect to child pornography this is less often considered—the pornography itself. Since the early days of modern photography, skilled craftsmen could manipulate photographs in order to deceive the viewer. Transposition of bodies and juxtaposition of surroundings are all photo-manipulation techniques that should be of no surprise to the reader.

The digital age of imaging has enhanced the photographer's ability to fool the viewer's eye. Photo-manipulation tools grow more powerful with each generation, and three-dimensional imaging programs offer totally spurious creations that are almost indistinguishable from genuine images. Eventually, if not currently, completely computer-generated images will be indistinguishable from those depicting a real-life event.

In the world of child pornography, this fact has raised a previously hidden problem—what of computer-generated child pornography? Regardless of the reader's personal belief about the rights of people to do as they please, this issue is one that the courts will have to wrestle with, and one whose outcome is not entirely predictable. The legality of an image created entirely in the digital realm, using no children in its creation, is somewhat unclear. While many of the traditional reasons for outlawing child pornography still exist, some do not. For example, no children are harmed during the making of digital child pornography; as a result, there is no way to establish the legal requirement of proving the actor in the photo—or video—is under the legal age. It may sound like a minor technicality, but it may prove a high hurdle to overcome in the future.

CONCEALMENT

Child pornographers can now harness the power of computers to conceal illegal images for storage and transmission using steganography. They can encrypt their cache of "goodies" using high-powered cryptographic programs, and they can share their love of the illegal with others through Internet chat rooms and anonymous e-mail transmissions. Fortunately, the "good guys" can also harness the power of computer technology to try to combat this threat to children.

Many police agencies have embraced the technology and have begun turning the power of the chat room, blogs, and file transfer sites against predators. A number of agencies, including several federal government law enforcement agencies, are aggressively pursuing predators by posing as children in these chat rooms and engaging in instant message exchange with predators in hopes of ensnaring them in their own game of cat and mouse.[10]

Within the confines of the rules regarding entrapment, police officers are patrolling the Internet, watching and waiting for predators to take the bait. When they do, an often tedious series of thrust and parries ensues in which the police attempt to entice predators, without really enticing them, into making the fateful move of meeting in person. This final phase, known as the face-to-face (F2F in computer parlance), usually results in the arrest of the predator who is usually quite shocked that the 12-year-old girl he thought he was meeting for sex is in reality a 44-year-old overweight detective.

Creative agencies have begun exploring other ways of ensnaring predators and tracking their movement. No discussion of the impact that computers have had on criminal behavior would be complete without at least mentioning the offender databases that are in place in nearly every state in the nation. These databases contain the names, and usually the photographs, of every sex offender in the state. The databases are cross-referenced by address, and allow citizens to search by address and find out exactly what predators may be living around their neighborhood. The database maintained by the Florida Department of Law Enforcement is an good example of this (www3.fdle.state.fl.us/sopu/index.asp).

Not without their critics, these databases have been heralded as a great way to raise public awareness about predatory behavior. Regardless of whether you are for or against the registration of sex offenders and public access to the database, it is beyond dispute that in this area computer technology has greatly impacted criminal behavior.

AUCTION FRAUD AND RETAIL CONS

Internet auction fraud is a phenomenon that can only be attributable to the Internet. Before the rise of the Internet, there was no such thing as an online auction. While eBay (www.ebay.com) and other popular online auction sites have revolutionized the way people sell personal belongings, they have also opened up an entirely new venue for hucksters to ply their trade.

Internet auctions work similar to real-world auctions. A seller places an item up for sale, and interested buyers bid against each other until bidding closes. Then the highest bidder walks away with what could be a phenomenal bargain—or a colossal rip-off.

In the online auction setting, the traditional auction house is replaced by the online service provider. In the case of the eBay, the company acts as both a storehouse of the information and a venue for the bidding. Not a retailer itself, eBay merely serves as an intermediary and a venue through which the underlying sales transactions occur. As eBay has grown, the services it provides have increased, and currently it offers a number of ancillary services that help to enhance the buying and selling of items.

Although the concept of online auctions began as a sort of Internet garage sale, it has evolved into an entirely new retail paradigm. From the humble beginnings where private sellers used online auctions as a way of cheaply unloading an attic full of junk, online auctions have evolved into a futuristic consignment shop and profitable extension to brick-and-mortar businesses.

In today's online auction world, buyers are as likely to be confronted by a sales pitch from a major retailer as they are an offer to buy Grandma's priceless Hummel figurine. Retailers big and small have embraced the auction paradigm as a way to enter the world of online sales. In many cases, the investment necessary to begin retailing through online auctions is much less than that necessary to establish a true web presence with all the additional administration problems that brings. Retailers have discovered that the international reach of the online auction house is a cost-effective way to increase the geographic reach of their land-based business.

As beneficial as this may be for retailers, with it comes opportunity for new forms of fraud. Internet auction fraud takes several different forms, but the most common complaints probably center on merchandise that is purchased (or won) and never arrives. Other problems involve "bait-and-switch" frauds in which the merchandise pictured is a false representation of the actual product shipped. Additionally, the use of shills has been noted as being a serious concern.[11]

Shills artificially inflate the bidding on a particular item. Since selling and bidding are semianonymous in the online auction world, sellers can create multiple user accounts. Using the first account, the seller places an item online for bidding. Then, logging in using another account, the same seller either begins the bidding at an artificially high price point or waits until other legitimate bidders have begun bidding, and then drives the price up by bidding against them.

Anyone who has participated in an online auction can confirm that for popular items, the bidding war that occurs during the final few seconds of an item's open bid period rivals the most rousing exchange among bidders at brick-and-mortar auction houses. In my experience, it is not uncommon for bid prices to increase by 150 to 200 percent during the final minutes of bidding. Inject a shill into the mix and the reader can easily see how what began as a true bargain ends as an overpriced rip-off.

Fortunately, the major online auction providers put an end to this type of fraud fairly quickly. In effort to combat seller fraud further, most sites have instituted a feedback system. Given the volume of buyers and sellers on most online auction sites, it would be impossible for the auction to verify each and every seller, let alone both the sellers and all bidders. Using the feedback system, participants help to step in to fill the void.

In the feedback system, the auction provider verifies the identity of each buyer and seller (usually by ensuring that there is a valid e-mail address, some other minor vital information, and no other account exists using the same e-mail address to protect against shills). From that point forward, participants in the auction community are responsible for policing themselves.

When a seller and buyer consummate a transaction, the buyer is asked to provide feedback about the seller and how the transaction went. Good and bad feedback is tabulated for that seller and becomes part of the public information on the site. The more positive transactions sellers have, the higher their feedback rating is. That way, buyers can feel more comfortable doing business with that seller. Similar feedback is posted for buyers.

Additional buyer protection is often implemented by using outside payment brokerage services. These services act as a sort of escrow service between buyers and sellers, and often take some of the fear out of paying for merchandise sight unseen. Taken together, these safeguards can make online auctions a fairly safe form of business transaction.

In addition to auction fraud, online retail fraud is also a possibility. Many of the problems just discussed are present in any retail transaction consummated entirely online. Bait and switch, failure to ship merchandise, and identity theft are all very real problems that confront computer users who are contemplating doing business online. While no amount of protection will guarantee a safe shopping experience, common sense and a dose of skepticism can greatly reduce the potential for victimization.

Law enforcement agencies, by and large, handle most online fraud scenarios no differently from those that occur in the real world, and in most cases, laws that protect consumers in brick-and-mortar transactions can be applied to online transactions. The difficulty that online transaction adds is the collection of the digital evidence.

As Chapter 2 highlights, the preservation and collection of digital evidence involves some unique concerns. In a traditional fraud involving a retail transaction, production of an invoice or sales receipt is pretty straightforward. In an online transaction, not only does production of the invoice become problematic, but what actually constitutes an invoice is often up to debate. Further confusing the issue is the fact that identifying parties to transactions online is sometimes difficult. In the semi-anonymous world of computers and the Internet, identifying a unique individual behind a screen name is not impossible, but can be nearly so.

Hiding behind proxy servers and using anonymous remailers, Internet fraudsters can thwart all but the most dedicated computer forensic investigators who unflaggingly leapfrog from IP (Internet Protocol) address to IP address until the suspect's real-world address is finally uncovered. Many times this real-world address ends up being in a location far outside the jurisdiction of the original investigator. When this happens, interagency cooperation becomes essential. Making matters worse in that case are those situations in which the laws or entire legal systems are different among the jurisdictions. When this happens, successful prosecution becomes a much less likely outcome.

Fortunately, many nations and all states in the United States have entered an era of cooperation when it comes to online fraud. Recognizing that these interagency problems are bound to arise more and more frequently, many jurisdictions have formed task forces and entered into explicit agreements about how cases that cross borders will be handled.

COUNTERFEITING AND FORGERY

Among the many traditional crimes that have found their way into the digital world, forgery and counterfeiting may have received the greatest technological boost. In the old days of counterfeiting, highly skilled artists slaved over metal plates for seemingly endless hours in order to duplicate the fine detail present in printed U.S. currency. True counterfeiters were both criminals and artists whose skills were often respected by the authorities who pursued them.

When the computer entered the picture, high school pranksters became the newest threat to the U.S. Secret Service. High-quality color scanners and laser printers began to turn out nearly perfect copies of U.S. currency that were able to pass casual scrutiny with surprising regularity. These new age counterfeiters did not limit themselves to currency either. They quickly learned that computers could duplicate checks with equal facility—and passing counterfeit checks was not a federal crime.

Using the tools that nearly every home now possessed, perfect copies of payroll checks, personal checks, and business checks became a common occurrence. This increase gave rise to greater attention to the quality of both U.S. currency and checks.

The U.S. Treasury, partly in response to the newly minted threat of computer technology, began a program of overhauling the security features on U.S. currency. Special features such as microprinting are now included. Microprinting is microscopically small print that can be produced only using highly detailed printing plates. Most consumer-level scanners and printers lack the resolution detail necessary to duplicate microprinting reliably and accurately.

Another security feature incorporated into currency is the embedded metallic strip. All redesigned currency contains a security strip with the denomination of the bill imprinted on it. This strip is embedded in the fibers of the paper, not printed on top. Again, the incorporation of the strip into the paper itself makes computer duplication impossible.[12]

Likewise, many of the features such as microprinting and embedded security features that we see in U.S. currency are also incorporated into most draft instruments, such as checks and money orders.

PROSTITUTION

Even the sex trade has benefited from the growth of computer technology. Traditional prostitutes have begun moving their operations into the cyberworld. Realizing the marketing benefits of Internet storefronts, high-class escort services and street-level prostitution operations both have an Internet presence. As an investigator I personally worked such a case.

In this case, the Web site brazenly trumpeted its services with very little attempt to conceal the true nature of the business, and listed photographs and biographies of a number of women. Several of these women were under legal age and were specifically marketed to clients preferring young girls. All "dates" were arranged through e-mail transactions and booked in advance. Several times every month, the site's owner transported the girls to out-of-town locations to meet with repeat customers or new clients willing to pay the travel fee, which sometimes topped $3,000.

When the operation was finally dismantled, thousands of e-mails were recovered from clients throughout the United States arranging for "dates." Additionally, as is often the case in prostitution, the owner of the service was also heavily involved in narcotics distribution.

SECURITIES FRAUD

One area that is sometimes overlooked when discussing computer crime is the role that computers play in securities fraud. Although not as common as other forms of fraud, fraudulent activity involving publicly traded securities has the potential to result in hundreds of thousands of dollars in losses to businesses and victims.

One of the areas in which computer technology has the potential to impact securities transactions is in a market manipulation scheme. In this scheme, which has already been documented, a stock manipulator posts spurious information about a particular stock in an Internet chat room with the intention of influencing the sale of that stock. The power of this scheme lies in the willingness of consumers to look for a bargain anywhere possible.[13]

As recent insider trading cases have shown us, many people will not balk at the chance to either earn a few extra dollars or to reduce their losses by a few pennies. Capitalizing on this foible of human nature, stock fraudsters post messages that purport to contain inside information about a particular stock. If the news heralds an impending yet not publicly disclosed discovery, the stock will obviously grow in value. Conversely, if the news foretells an adverse event for the stock, the price will drop. Depending on the manipulator's position, he or she will then either buy or sell holdings to make a tidy profit.

This scheme depends in large part in how believable the posting is and how quickly the momentum of the information can grow. Obviously, if the momentum grows slowly, the likelihood of discovery increases and the fraudster's ability to consummate the deal is destroyed. In some cases, the information does not even need to be accurate. What is most important, from a legal standpoint, is that the information is not public and is being used to effect or influence a market activity. In these cases, the market was manipulated, or the attempt was made to manipulate the market.

An example of this form of market manipulation is seen in the case of Jonathan Lebed. Lebed used hundreds of postings and a dozen fictitious names to inflate the value of nine different stocks. Using the various names and multitude of postings, Lebed was able to add an air of credibility to his postings and succeeded in influencing the market for his target stock. In the end he profited to the tune of over $275,000. Perhaps more amazing than the ease with which Lebed pulled off this scheme was the fact that at the time of the offense, he was only 15 years old.[14] As web blogs and Internet chat room popularity continues to grow, it is likely that these types of securities fraud will also grow.

No discussion of crime and technology would be complete without at least mentioning cyberstalking, or harassment of a person using the Internet. Most often the preferred method for cyberstalking is through e-mail. Techniques like mail bombs, where the victim's inbox is flooded with hundreds of large e-mail messages, can make the victim's cyberlife miserable. Additionally, cyberstalkers may send third parties messages with forged return addresses making them appear to have come from the stalking victim's account. Finally, one of the more troubling aspects of cyberstalking is online harassment.[15]

In this case, the suspect uses anonymous postings on Web sites, blogs, and chat rooms to defame and disparage the victim. The resulting harm to the victim's reputation can have long-term emotional effects and in some cases can ruin the victim professionally.

In recent years, law enforcement has begun to take cases of cyberstalking more seriously. No longer are victims told that there is nothing that police can do. In fact, some states, such as Florida, have enacted specific statutes targeting harassing online behavior. In Florida, Chapter 784.048 explicitly makes harassment by electronic communication a crime. This broadly written law defines cyberstalking as follows:

> to engage in a course of conduct to communicate, or to cause to be communicated, words, images, or language by or through the use of electronic mail or electronic communication, directed at a specific person, causing substantial emotional distress to that person and serving no legitimate purpose. [16]

Similar statutes have been implemented in many states and have led to much greater law enforcement response to the growing problem.

Last, our discussion focuses on a problem that some consider less a criminal issue than a problem with a capitalistic society—piracy.

With the emergence of digital technology, copying music and video files has been catapulted to the front of societies' consciousness. While teenagers have been copying music since the advent of inexpensive tape recording technology, the digital revolution has changed the landscape in ways that most people do not readily appreciate.

In the analog world of cassette tapes and LP albums, copies become degraded with each new generation. Even with high-quality analog recording equipment, the nature of the beast means that the first copy of the original will be of lower quality than the original. The second copy will be worse than the first copy, and so on down the line. This is an inherent limitation of the medium. Because of this limitation, the commercial music world was not greatly concerned about the phenomenon of music sharing, even though it has been going on for years. The digital revolution has turned the commercial music industry on its head.

In the digital world, copies of digital files are "perfect copies." Because we are merely transferring a series of 0s and 1s, there is absolutely no appreciable loss of quality. Add to this perfect image the fact that the copy process is usually much faster than the copy process of years gone by, and you have a recipe for abuse.

In the 1970s, when you wanted to copy an album to cassette or dub a cassette, you usually had to play the entire album or cassette from start to finish. In today's digital world, most copying is done in a bit-stream format, which means that it is not a real-time process but occurs in the much faster digital world. In most cases, depending on the speed and format of the hardware, an entire music CD can be copied in under 15 minutes.

Movie files have only added fuel to the fire. Because digital movies are essentially the same as music files, differing only in format, the same advantages as those seen in digital music copying are realized in movie file copying. Exact bit-for-bit transfers mean zero loss of quality. Gone are the days of the grainy, jittery VHS tape copies we became accustomed to in the last two decades.

The speed and ease with which these files can be copied and their quality mean that consumers have a tremendous incentive to participate in file-sharing networks where perfect copies can be exchanged for free. This is where some people begin to see this as a consumer issue, not a legal issue.

Some argue that the high price of music and movies justify the sharing of these resources among consumers and that instead of responding with legislation, the responsibility for dealing with the problem lies in market forces and the "invisible hand" of the marketplace. Regardless of the position you take on this issue, the fact remains that lawmakers have made the decision to make file sharing and distribution of copyrighted movies and music illegal.

Given that fact, the burden often falls on computer forensic investigators to search for evidence of file sharing and piracy of copyrighted software and media files. In pursuing this type of case, investigators must have a working knowledge of how file-sharing or peer-to-peer (P2P) networks operate.

Peer-to-peer is a system for exchanging files among computer users. In one of the early implementations of this protocol, a program known as Napster revolutionized the way people traded files. The theory behind Napster is relatively simple. Users download client software that they install on their computer. One of the jobs of the client software is to search users' hard drives for music files (with the permission of users). The other job of the client is to share this information with the main server program.[17]

Once several users have downloaded the client software and installed it on their computers, they can log into the server and search for music files. While the files themselves do not actually reside on the server's computer, pointers to the computer addresses of fellow network members do. In that way, a user searching for a particular file can query the server, which responds with the address where the file can be located. The requesting user then connects directly with the computer user who has the file, and the exchange is made. Under this paradigm for file sharing, the server acts as nothing more than a referral service, pointing requesting users in the direction of users who have the filed being requested.

Ingenious as it is, this method of sharing music files was eventually held to be illegal as a form of copyright infringement—because the majority of the files being shared were copyright-protected music files.[18]

Although Napster has subsequently taken the high road and begun marketing MP3 music files legally in a joint venture with a number of record labels, the proverbial cat was out of the bag. After the U.S. Court of Appeals for the Ninth Circuit declared Napster's service a facilitator of copyright infringement. Napsters popularity began to decline. Subsequently, similar systems, with slightly different methodologies and offshore ownership, arose to fill the void. Sites like www.gnutella.com and www.kazaa.com have attempted to carry on the torch first lit by Napster.[19]

Peer-to-peer is not the only way in which copyrighted files are shared. Services such as Internet Relay Chat (IRC) (www.irc.org), a form of web chat, and usenet newsgroups are very popular destinations for consumers looking to download files.

Usenet newsgroups are loosely aligned collections of users who join together and post messages containing files that other users can download. Regardless of whether the uploaded file is a movie, music, or computer software file, a dedicated channel to trade it exists among the literally tens of thousands of channels.[20] The popularity of file sharing, whether done on a P2P basis or by downloading from newsgroups or IRC channels and File Transfer Protocol[21] (FTP) sites, will continue to grow as the cost of music, movies, and software increases.

CONCLUSION

In this chapter, I have touched on some of the many ways in which computers and digital technology have insinuated themselves into the criminal realm (or, perhaps, the criminal realm has insinuated itself into the world of digital technology). Either way, the result is the same: Computers and digital technology have impacted criminal investigations in previously unforeseen ways.

Although crime has been around much longer than digital technology, both areas have merged to present new challenges to computer forensic investigators. Some of these challenges require investigators to think outside the predefined realm of experience and employ creative solutions to problems.

In the next chapter, I offer further insight into how investigators employ computer technology to tackle the new challenges of computer-literate criminals. The topics covered include not only forensic examination tools but also more mainstream computer software and tools that investigators can easily adapt to investigations with computer overtones.

NOTES

1. Federal Trade Commission (FTC), "Identity Theft Victim Complaint Data: Figures and Trends June 5, 2006." Available at: www.consumer.gov/idtheft/pdf/clearinghouse_2005.pdf.
2. Robert Moore, *Cybercrime: Investigating High-Technology Computer Crime* (Cincinnati, OH: Anderson Publishing, 2005), pp. 63–64.
3. Ibid., pp. 64–65.
4. Ibid., pp. 66–67.
5. See U.S. Department of Justice Press Release, "Federal Charges Filed Against 21 Persons for Trafficking in Stolen and Counterfeit Credit

Cards," May 27, 2004. Available at: www.usdoj.gov/usao/nv/home/
pressrelease/may2004/iancu052704.htm.

6. FTC, "Identity Theft Victim Complaint Data."

7. See generally FTC, "FTC Consumer Alert: How Not to Get Hooked
   by a Phishing Scam. June 5, 2006." Available at: www.ftc.gov/
   bcp/conline/pubs/alerts/phishingalrt.pdf.

8. Anti-Phishing Working Group, "Phishing Attack Trends Report" (March
   2004). Available at: www.antiphishing.org/reports/APWG_Phishing_
   Attack_Report-Mar2004.pdf.

9. Hope Yen, "Veteran's Group Sues over Data Theft," MSNBC.Com,
   June 6, 2006. Available at: www.msnbc.msn.com/id/13168240/

10. CBS News, "Online Child Porn Ring Smashed: Sting Operation Leads
    to 27 Arrests in U.S. and Three Other Countries," March 15,
    2006. Available at: www.cbsnews.com/stories/2006/03/15/national/
    main1406067.shtml.

11. See FTC, "Internet Auctions: A Guide for Buyers and Sellers. June 15,
    2006." Available at: www.ftc.gov/bcp/conline/pubs/online/auctions.
    pdf.

12. U.S. Bureau of Engraving and Printing, "Counterfeit Deterrence.
    June 5, 2006." http://origin.moneyfactory.com/newmoney/files/Fact_
    Sheets_Combined/Deterrence.pdf.

13. See Judith Burns, "E-Mail, Chat Rooms, Bulletin Boards Provide Invit-
    ing Spot for Stock Fraud," *Wall Street Journal*, November 18, 1998.
    See also Christine Souhrada, "Securities Fraud, Market Manipulation,
    and the Internet," *UCLA Journal of Law and Technology*, Notes 28
    (2002). Available at: www.lawtechjournal.com/notes/2002/28_020829_
    souhrada.php.

14. Souhrada, "Securities Fraud."

15. Moore, *Cybercrime*, pp. 113–116.

16. *Florida State Statutes Annotated*, Title XLVI Chapter 784.048
    sec. (1)(d). (West 2006).

17. Moore, *Cybercrime*, pp. 119–124; see also Eoghan Casey, *Digital
    Evidence and Computer Crime: Forensic Science, Computers and the
    Internet* (Boston: Elsevier, 2004), pp. 57–62.

18. *A&M Records, Inc. v. Napster, Inc.*, 114 F.Supp. 2d 896 (N.D.Cal.,
    2000).

19. Richard Menta, "Napster Clones Crush Napster," MP3Newswire.net,
    July 20, 01. Available at: www.mp3newswire.net/stories/2001/
    topclones.html.

20. Wikipedia contributors, "Usenet," *Wikipedia, The Free Encyclopedia,* http://en.wikipedia.org/w/index.php?title=Usenet&oldid=77845175.

21. File Transfer Protocol is a computer technology for transferring files among computer users regardless of the underlying operating system. FTP allows users of MAC, PC or UNIX systems to share files irrespective of their operating system.

8

COMPUTER TOOLS AND THE FORENSIC EXAMINATION

INTRODUCTION

In this chapter, I discuss some of the wide variety of tools that computer forensic investigators use. In order to make the operation of these tools more clear, I discuss them in the context of a particular computer forensic examination. Many of these tools were developed specifically for use by computer forensic investigators. Others were developed for other areas of computer security and have, over time, been modified to serve the unique needs of forensic investigators. Still others have been developed for consumer use, and have been adapted over time to serve the needs of forensic investigators.

Like any list, this one is far from complete. Tools you may have heard or even used may not appear. That does not mean they are any less valuable to computer investigators. I have listed what I believe are the most frequently used tools by investigators. Also, just because a tool is in this section does not necessarily mean it is the best or most popular tool. Instead, you should view this chapter as an introduction to some of the tools that are available.

ASSUMING CONTROL OF THE CASE

When computer forensic investigators assume control of a case from a criminal investigator, the first thing they must do is evaluate the case. This evaluation should be done during a meeting with the criminal investigator. During this meeting forensic investigators begin collecting information about things such as the authority for the search and its scope. They also must consider the potential for additional, nondigital evidence collection procedures, such as fingerprinting or trace evidence recovery and assessment of the suspect's skill level.

Depending on whether the investigators have been retained by a law enforcement agency or by a private party, authorization to search may be granted through such procedures as search warrants, civil production orders, or even voluntary consent. Regardless of the manner in which authorization is received, this key element of the examination must be established; otherwise, all the tedious work that follows will be for nothing.

UNDERSTANDING THE CASE

Understanding the background of the case can make the job of investigators more focused. This phase of the assessment requires investigators to function more like traditional detectives. Exploring questions about things such as the nature of the offense, the skill level of the offender, and the sophistication of the computer installation may help narrow the scope of search and might even suggest new search methodologies.

Once the initial evaluation is complete, investigators must evaluate the scene, taking into consideration things such as the type and number of computers, the type of documentation, existence of proprietary software, and particular pieces of hardware that might present logistical problems during the seizure. One such hardware consideration is large-format hard drives. Current storage technology makes the probability of encountering terabyte-size hard drives something investigators must consider. By recognizing this fact before initiating the seizure, investigators can avoid last-minute problem solving.

As part of the on-scene evaluation, investigators will make some judgment calls. One such call will focus on whether the collection of digital evidence should be done on scene or in the laboratory. As a rule, the best-case scenario for any evidence collection process, digital or not, is in a controlled environment. The safe, secure, and digitally sterile environment of the computer forensic lab is always the ideal place to collect evidence. Sometimes the ideal is not possible. Some circumstances that make on-site collection the only viable option are networked data storage, RAID (redundant array of independent disks) arrays, and the nature of the business under investigation.

For example, if the business for which the search authorization has been granted is a newspaper publisher, seizing the system and transporting it to a secure location triggers a number of legal concerns, including First Amendment issues that may best be avoided at all costs, regardless of the strength of your case.

EVALUATING THE EVIDENCE

After the scene has been assessed and documented, investigators must evaluate the evidence itself. Taking care to document in detail every phase of this process, investigators will begin to inventory the individual components of the system, evaluating external storage media such as CD-Rs and DVDs, and examining peripheral devices. By carefully examining the individual components of the system, investigators can begin to understanding the best way to approach the seizure. Once this external examination of the scene and the system itself is complete, investigators must once again rely on experience and best judgment in deciding how to proceed next.

One of the tasks computer forensic specialists face is collecting volatile data from a live system. As I discussed in earlier chapters, the possibility of collecting volatile data brings with it the problem of changing system information. As you will recall, any action investigators take necessarily changes information in the volatile memory and likely in the hard disk storage as well. Sometimes, however, the side effect of changing information is justified by the particularities of the investigation. If that is the case, then investigators are faced with the task of collecting the data from multiple sources on the running system in the least intrusive way possible.

EXAMINING THE "LIVE" SYSTEM

As I have warned repeatedly, the very act of observing the system changes the system. Therefore, anything investigators do in this process will change the system. With that in mind, commercial products such as Encase (www. guidancesoftware.com) and ProDiscover from Technology Pathways (www. techpathways.com) offer investigators powerful ways to collect data from running systems. Such data includes running processes, users and programs, as well as network connections and physical configuration of the system itself.

One option that these powerful tools offer investigators is the ability to collect information in a networked environment. The Enterprise edition of Encase and ProDiscover allow users to connect to a remote system and conduct a live examination of the processes and files running on the system. This feature becomes even more important in light of the potential for rootkit activity.

As discussed in Chapter 6, rootkits are Trojan horse–type programs that seize control of computers at the system level. As such, they offer computer intruders a very powerful way of concealing their presence and covering their tracks. Their power makes collecting information from a live system somewhat more difficult.

There are three generations of rootkits in circulation. The first generation rootkit (also known as a file system rootkit), which has been around perhaps from the early 1960s, simply replaces the DOS "DIR" command with a Trojaned version. The "DIR" command, when typed in the command line, returns an entire listing of computer files on that hard drive. Even though it is rudimentary by today's standards, it is an effective way of uncovering an intruder. The earliest Trojaned "DIR" executables altered the information that the command returned, deleting all references to hacker files and utilities, making them invisible to users. The only listings users uncovered were those files the intruder wished users to see.[1]

Second-generation rootkits built on this concept but added more power to the program. These programs, called library rootkits because they are designed to highjack library files (files with the. dll (which stands for dynamic linked library) extension that are included as function libraries with computer programs). Nearly all computer programs rely on library files in order to execute. Library files make programming much more compartmentalized and fit well with the object-oriented approach to most Windows programming languages. For example, if a programmer is writing a complicated software program that requires many complex math subroutines for proper execution, instead of embedding the same math subroutine fifteen times in the main body of the program, he can simply encapsulate all the math subroutines in a library file, from which they can be called from anywhere in the main program. Library files also add portability to computer programs.

If a programmer envisions a program being distributed in multiple languages, all the text and user messages can be encapsulated in the library file. When a message box needs text to display a message to the user, it simply fetches it from the library file and plugs it into the box. Swapping library files containing foreign-language text is much easier than recoding the entire program.

The Windows operating system (OS) utilizes library files extensively and in much the same manner. When the OS needs information from the system, it calls a subroutine from within a .dll file. The subroutine fetches the information and returns it to the OS. In the case of a rootkit that operates at the library level, the hacker replaces the Windows' .dll with a Trojaned version that reports to the OS only the system information that the hacker wishes. The library-level rootkit operates very similarly to the first-generation rootkit. One of the most widely used and successful second-generation rootkits is a program known as Hacker Defender (http://hxdef.org/).[2]

Third-generation rootkits are also known as kernel-mode rootkits because they operate at the command kernel level. They take the library rootkit concept one very powerful step forward. As mentioned, when Windows needs information from the system, it usually enlists the help of a function call in a library. If the library has been corrupted, the integrity of the information returned by the function call cannot be trusted. Since the rootkit returns only the information the hacker wants it to, the backdoor process the hacker installed on the computer remains hidden from the OS. This is a powerful ploy, but it is vulnerable because investigators can get accurate system information by bypassing the library function call.

Kernel-mode rootkits take away that power. A kernel-mode rootkit highjacks the command kernel itself through a process known as hooking (www.rootkit.com).[3] This very sophisticated solution then returns only the information the hacker wants returned—at the system level. Every program, including forensic examination tools that call on the system for information, will be fed the corrupted data. This ability provides near invisibility for the hacker and would appear to be an impenetrable ruse—but fortunately, it is not.[4]

Two powerful forensic examination techniques have been developed to allow investigators to identify systems that have been compromised by kernel-mode rootkits. They should be used in combination and can effectively identify rootkits that are running on a target system.

First, examiners must access the target computer system from a remote, "trusted" system. This is where the network capabilities of tools such as Encase Enterprise and ProDiscover are valuable. Second, investigators compare the hash value of the system files with the hash value of trusted binaries. Hashing is a simple concept with a very complicated implementation. It is the key to many aspects of computer forensics and, therefore, deserves a few paragraphs of explanation.

At its most basic, hashing can be conceptualized as the equivalent of a fingerprint. In real-world investigations, it is scientifically accepted that no two persons have identical fingerprints. Notwithstanding recent speculation by several experts to the contrary, this belief makes it possible for me to say with scientific certainty that the fingerprints at the crime scene were left by the suspect. The internal integrity of the structure of the fingerprint makes it so.

Digital fingerprinting, or hashing, creates a unique (to a scientific certainty) hash value, which will always be the same for that particular digital object.[5] As an example, let us examine a digital photograph. Every photograph, as you recall, is nothing more than a collection of 0s and 1s. The file is processed using a hashing program, and each bit of data is evaluated. A unique number is produced on the other end of the program. This number, the hash value, will always be the same, every time the program is run on that file, no matter how many times the file is copied or printed. The power of the hash is that no other file, regardless of how closely it resembles the original, will ever have the same hash value. Just like no two people will ever have the same fingerprints, the hash value of any image will uniquely identify the file forever.

The added beauty of the hash process, aside from verifying the chain of custody (which will be discussed shortly) is that any change in the original image file will produce an entirely different hash value—even if only one bit is changed. By comparing the two hash values, investigators can tell instantly that one of the two files have been altered. In addition to offering the ability to verify the authenticity of a file for evidentiary purposes, hashing helps us solve the rootkit problem.

Hashes can be run on all sorts of digital objects: images, documents, computer programs, libraries, binary files, even entire hard drives. Because of this, we can obtain the hash value of all the Windows system programs, kernel binary files, and Windows library files. Since hash values never change, the hash value from the original library file in a Windows "clean" system should match the hash value of a suspect library file on an unknown system. In the rootkit example, a database of all Windows programs and many other popular programs contains all the "true" hash values. Hashing all the program files on the target computer and comparing their values to the trusted values in the database allows investigators to identify compromised files.

Therefore, one of the first things computer investigators do when examining a live system is check the hash values of all the files on the system and compare them to known hash values. In addition to OS file values, there are also databases that contain hash values for known hacker files. Using many of the advanced investigation suites, investigators can search the hard drive comparing the hash value of each file on the drive to the database of known hacker programs. Even if the name of the file has been changed, the hash value stays the same. This hashing process has been extended to other areas as well.

In child pornography cases, certain images files tend to circulate frequently and seem to be perennial images in most predators' collections. Investigators have compiled databases of hash values for these common images files. Much like the preceding example, investigators can compare the hash values of individual files on the target computer with the database of known pornographic images. A match proves to a scientific certainty that the image, regardless of the name, is the contraband file.

Now that we have a way around the rootkit problem, we can discuss the data investigators are likely to find in a search of volatile memory.

Volatile information is stored in a number of places in a computer such as cache files and routing tables. Investigators are often interested in these cache files, routing tables, and process tables because they contain valuable information about the configuration of the computer itself and which processes are running. However, other things may be of greater significance.

System memory may contain bits and chunks of programs, images, and documents. What is more, it may contain all or part of the user's password for particular programs. In fact, when a user types a password into the Mozilla browser, six copies of that password are stored in various locations on the computer system. These hidden passwords can save investigators hours or weeks of work. In some cases, they could spell the difference between success and failure, since some forms of computer encryption are, practically speaking, unbreakable. In addition, systems running the Microsoft Encrypted File System (EFS) cache the file being encrypted in memory—in plain text. A search of system memory could result in recovery of an entire unencrypted file that would otherwise be unrecoverable.

Even when cached passwords are associated with programs of little interest to investigators directly, human nature tells us that the same passwords may be reused in other programs. Keeping this in mind, careful investigators always treat every password as a hidden jewel.

In general terms, the information that investigators are looking for on a live system are:

- *Network information.* Data about the IP (Internet Protocol) address, route tables, installed networking protocols, and devices connected to the system are all valuable bits of information.
- *Date and time information.* At first glance, the importance of this information may be missed; however, as the investigation moves forward, it is very important to match system time with real-world time. Placing suspects or defendants at the computer during key moments in time can be the crux of a case. These pieces of data are available and include things such as time zone settings and daylight savings time settings.
- *Running processes.* This includes information about what processes and code are running on the system at the time of the seizure. An obvious problem with this information exists if an undetected rootkit is hidden on the system. The accuracy of information when a rootkit is running is suspect at best.
- *User information.* This information includes data about the users currently logged into the system, both locally and remotely, and in some cases, recent login attempts and failures.
- *System scheduling.* System scheduling information tells about pending tasks or scheduled processes that are awaiting completion or in process. This information can be a valuable clue as to what system processes the target routinely runs, and may lead to location of other programs or files of interest.

The value of this information to investigations of cyberattack or intrusion is obvious. While not quite as obvious, its value in stand-alone cases is also great. Many times the difference between success and failure of an investigation lies in the investigators' ability to place the suspect "at the keyboard." While not bulletproof, evidence from volatile memory that shows the suspect was logged in to the system at the time and date of seizure could be the difference in the case. Likewise, knowing that the system time and date were different on two different computers on a network could make synchronizing data much easier.

Therefore, balancing what may be lost with what investigators are likely to uncover will guide them in their decision as to whether collection of volatile data from a live system is worthwhile. In some cases, live collection will not even be an option if the computer system is powered off when investigators arrive.

COLLECTING DATA FROM A DEAD SYSTEM

Regardless of whether investigators collect live data and power down the computer or the computer is off to begin with, eventually collection of the stored data will become necessary. Again, proceeding on instinct and training, investigators often plan the collection process to best fit the given scenario.

In the initial phases of the examination, investigators have documented the configuration and connections of the computer system. As the internal examination begins, the documentation process continues. As a first step, investigators likely remove the computer cover and document the location and type of system components. Identifying information about hard drives, memory configuration, and additional user-added peripheral devices such as hardware RAID controllers can offer valuable clues about the skill level of the suspect.

Additionally, manufacturer data about the hard drives can help investigators compare the manufacturer's stated storage capacity to the capacity recognized by the system. This could provide clues that hidden partitions have been created.

After collecting as much configuration information as possible, investigators will disconnect the hard drive(s) from the system board. As discussed in detail in Chapter 3, with the hard drives disconnected, investigators start the computer and enter the BIOS mode in order to record all the information contained in the BIOS. At this point, the information about the storage devices will be missing, since the hard drives have been disconnected. Instead, investigators record settings for the time, date, BIOS version number, and any other pertinent information about the system. Before exiting the BIOS setup utility, investigators change the boot-up sequence to instruct the system to look for an OS on either a floppy drive or a CD-ROM drive.

After changing and saving the settings, investigators insert the trusted boot floppy or CD they carry in their "forensic toolkit" and conduct a second controlled boot of the system. Note that the computer hard drives are still disconnected from the system board at this point. This is a precaution in case the changes to the BIOS were not made correctly or the forensic boot disk was not recognized. If the drives were plugged in before verifying the boot sequence and integrity of the boot CD, the system would automatically move to the installed hard drives looking for the OS. Looking for the OS will change data on the hard drive. Even if the change is only in file access times, this could compromise an investigator's ability to prove an element of the offense.

If the system properly boots from the controlled CD, investigators will turn the computer off and reconnect the hard drives. They will then do a third controlled boot-up with the forensic CD in the CD-ROM drive, access the BIOS/CMOS setup menu, and collect system information. This time, since the hard drives have been reinstalled, valuable information about the geometry of the disks is available. Using the information the system provides about drive configuration, number of sectors, and other disk parameters, investigators can compare the physical information from the manufacturer with the information listed by the system.

Since the proper settings have been verified and the forensic CD-ROM contains a software program known as a write-blocker, the computer system should not even access the installed hard drive.

Before moving on to the forensic acquisition of the drive, I want to discuss the forensic CD or floppy. The forensic boot floppy is a standard disk, either floppy or CD-R, that has been formatted to boot the system automatically. It contains the operating shell that will support basic fundamental functions of the system. In addition to a bare-bones version of operating software, the boot floppy will contain a number of forensic tools. The OS of choice is often MS-DOS 6.22, because of its compact size and power. Other systems can be used, such as earlier incarnations of the Windows OS. Recent versions, such as Windows 2000 and Windows XP, are not suitable for forensic work because of the lack of control they offer the user over system-level input/output I/O. In addition to a handful of operating system code called a stub, some or all of these programs may be found on a typical forensic boot floppy:

- Norton Disk Editor
- Hex Workshop
- Forensic acquisition tools such as:
  - DriveSpy
  - EnCase
  - SafeBack
  - SnapCopy
- Write-blocking software to protect the evidence drive

All these programs together usually fit on a 1.44 Mb floppy disk, making them very portable for investigators.

Although forensically tested write-blocking software has been proven to be an effective forensic solution for most cases, some investigators prefer a more robust method of preventing hard drive access; if so, they choose hardware-based write blockers.

A hardware-based write blocker controls access to the hard drive at the system level. In contrast to the software solution, which prevents software access by seizing control of particular interrupt calls, the hardware solution might be viewed as more fundamentally integrated into the system itself.

This hardware device plugs into the system board through the hard drive ribbon connector, and then the hard drive plugs into the write blocker. Although there are a number of manufacturers of these devices, they all work on the same fundamental principle: No information can be written to the disk.

One of the disadvantages of the hardware solution is that different configurations of disks may require different types of hardware write blockers. For example, ATA disks and SCSI disks may require two different hardware devices. Regardless of the drawbacks, hardware-based write blockers are very popular solutions to the problem of ensuring disk integrity. Most investigators use a combination of software and hardware write-blocking.

At this stage, experience once again helps investigators determine which avenue to choose. In some cases, it may be possible simply to disconnect the drives and transport them to the secure environment of the lab for imaging. In other situations, doing this may not be an option. Either at the lab or on the scene, investigators must capture an image of the drive. As I noted in earlier chapters, this can be the most precarious time in the investigation, given the potential for irrevocable damage to the sensitive digital evidence.

IMAGING THE DRIVE

Regardless of where the collection will occur, it will generally follow the same basic path. Once write protection is in place, investigators use one or more software solutions to transfer the information from the hard drive to their examination disk. Occasionally investigators may need to do some preliminary examination of the geometry of the disk. Perhaps there have been clues that the drive geometry has been intentionally altered, or perhaps there are concerns over imaging software compatibility that need to be answered before an imaging solution can be selected. Regardless, investigators may need to explore the drive, if only in a cursory manner.

Prior to initiating a capture, investigators should record the digital serial number of the drive and, unless the imaging software itself includes this function, create a hash of the entire drive. As discussed, hashes are very powerful tools. They can serve as fingerprints for all manner of digital objects, hard drives included. The purpose of hashing a drive before imaging is to ensure that investigators can attest to the data integrity after imaging. Investigators run a hashing algorithm on the drive. Given the nature of hashing, we accept as a scientific fact that if a single bit on the hashed drive changes, the hash value before the imaging operation will not match the hash value after the imaging operation. The hash serves to prove that the disk has not been altered in any way. It thus helps to establish a strong chain of custody. After the hash has been taken, investigators can image the drive using several options, both software and hardware based.

In the early days of computer forensics, hard drive imagers were limited to one or two programs that were not true "forensic" programs (meaning that they were developed as commercial products for applications other than forensic investigations). It just so happened that they worked well in this secondary role. One of the side effects of this phenomenon was that their early functionality was somewhat limited by today's standards. One of those limitations centered on drive size and geometry.

Luckily for law enforcement, the days of gigabyte drives were in the distant future, and terabyte-size disks were something from a science fiction movie. In fact, the first hard drive I ever imaged during an investigation was a whopping 10 megabytes—a veritable gargantuan warehouse back then, but not even a decent amount of on-board random access memory (RAM) today.

Today's software solutions have overcome nearly all the size and geometry limitations of their forefathers and in doing so have developed some truly dedicated followers. An added option of most modern disk imaging software is the ability to create a bit-stream image of the disk. A bit-stream image is slightly different from a raw bit-for-bit clone of the disk. It has advantages and disadvantages.

The advantage of a bit-stream image is that it can be broken into multiple storage units. For example, a 2-gigabyte (GB) hard drive image could be broken across four CD-Rs. Then, using imaging software, the image could be examined one disk at a time as if the entire image were continuous. One disadvantage is in instances where the imaging software itself cannot analyze a particular type of file, such as a Word format document, that file must be extracted to a raw-bit copy file and further processed with the appropriate software.

Another option confronting computer forensic investigators, and one that is very popular, is the hardware solution. Several leading manufacturers now provide turnkey solutions in handheld form. These imaging devices usually plug directly into the target drive and allow for capture of the image stream to an internal storage device. Some units can also be configured to work as a bridge between the target and a evidence disk. Additionally, many of these handheld solutions have incorporated some very high-level features, such as real-time keyword searching.

The MD5, manufactured by Logicube, allows users to insert a compact flash memory disk into the device. Users can load a list of keywords important to the investigation onto the card, and as the MD5 device transfers the target drive's data to the evidence drive, it simultaneously searches the information for matches to the keywords. This live search capability can cut investigative times into fractions of what they used to be. Additionally, the MD5 offers the ability to hash the drive before and after, and store that information with the evidence file for comparison.

Another stand-alone solution is the MyKey DriveCopy, which has built in write blocking and the option of a thermal printer to print out all the important data concerning both the target and evidence disks. There are new entrants to the handheld market each year. A relatively new addition to the hardware solution arena is the concept of the portable forensic workstation.

These workstations provide connectors for nearly every possible configuration of hard drives and come preloaded with the forensic software necessary for nearly any job. As one might expect, they are priced accordingly. One example of this sort of solution is the F.R.E.D. system.

F.R.E.D. stands for Forensic Recovery of Evidence Device and boasts the ability to handle any format hard drive, storage device, or thumb drive. In addition the F.R.E.D. has a 3.4-gigahertz (GHz) processor with 3 GB of RAM and 1.4 terabytes (TB) of hard drive storage space. Out of the box, the system has state-of-the-art forensic software installed and comes with optional hands-on training as part of the purchase price. F.R.E.D.'s creators, Digital Intelligence, have attempted to put everything forensic examiners could possibly need at their fingertips (www.digitalintelligence.com/products/fred/).

Regardless of whether investigators choose a software solution, a hardware solution, or perhaps a hybrid between the two, the imaging step ensures that a perfectly accurate bit-for-bit copy of the target drive is acquired on the evidence hard drive. Then, depending on the particulars of the case and agency policy, investigators most likely will duplicate the copy and store both the original target drive and the first copy in a secure evidence facility. All further analysis will be conducted on the second copy. This added level of protection simply ensures that the original evidence is far removed from the bit-by-bit examination that ultimately will change the nature of the data.

DATA EXTRACTION

Once the target drive has been imaged, the tedious job of extraction and analysis can begin. In this phase, computer forensic investigators first search the information on the drive, then determine what it all means. As discussed in earlier sections, the extraction of data often involves uncovering hidden data, recovering deleted files, and repairing damaged file structures. The extraction can occur at two levels: the physical and the logical.[6]

The search and extraction at the physical level allows investigators to search across the entire physical disk, regardless of the file structure. The logical search searches within the logical structure of the disk—that is, the file system and partition table. Both levels of search have their place, and each can be used in conjunction to accomplish investigators' goals.[7]

The physical extraction often begins with a keyword search in a forensic utility program such as Encase, FTK, or WinHex. Using the utility to search at the bit level, investigators search each inch of the disk for matching patterns and specific keywords. For example, in investigating employee embezzlement, investigators could search for specific terms that earlier conventional investigation methods had uncovered. Data such as phantom employee names, check amounts, check numbers, invoice names or items all make good keywords for searches.

By searching at the physical level using these powerful utilities, investigators can uncover data that may be hidden on the disk. Areas such as the host-protected area, hidden partitions, and falsely marked bad clusters are all open to search. Additionally, while in physical search and extraction mode, investigators are looking for mismatched partition information and errors in geometry and disk space. Because investigators are examining the disk at the bit-by-bit level, a strong knowledge of both disk geometry and hexadecimal numbers is helpful.

In the logical phase of the search, investigators are searching the disk at a higher level, using the OS file structure as a frame of reference. At this level, investigators will be looking at the file structure itself and searching for deleted files or files that may be misnamed, altered, or hidden. Investigators also are searching the file slack and any unallocated space on the disk. When both levels of search are concluded, investigators extract all recovered data to files that they can examine later, in the analysis phase.

During the extraction phase, investigators may be called on to break passwords, recover data through a method known as carving, and recover files that the system has marked as deleted.

As discussed earlier, the recovery process for deleted files can be straightforward. If the system has marked the file as a deleted file and has not yet written over any or all of the data, a simple file recover utility, such as the one provided by Norton Utilities, can easily extract the deleted file to a new file. However, if the system has already begun to reallocate the disk space for new files, the file's disk segments may have become fragmented, and some portions of the file may have already been overwritten. If so, the pointer system used to keep track of the individual file chunks is likely to have been disrupted, which makes automated recovery unlikely.

Carving utilities such as Foremost (http://foremost.sourceforge.net/), Win-Hex (www.x-ways.net/winhex/), and FTK (www.accessdata.com/) can automate the process of recovering these badly fragmented files. Although these tools help to automate the process of file carving and recovery, they are limited in their ability, and research is under way to create more robust and efficient carving tools. One such tool is Scalpel, which has some promise for providing an even more automated approach to what might otherwise be one of the most tedious tasks investigators face.[8] Imagine having to search an entire terabyte drive for tiny bits and pieces of a file—the phrase "needle in a haystack" comes immediately to mind. Once the extraction and recovery process is complete, investigators must analyze the data.

DATA ANALYSIS

Analysis is the stage of the forensic examination where the technician's data discovery and recovery skills merge with the skills of the investigator. Using the information obtained from the earlier stages in the forensic process, examiners now begin to try to figure out what it all means. In this stage the recovered information must be put into context so that some meaningful conclusions can be drawn. Analyzing the evidence occurs on many levels; however, most often it is done in these areas: time, hidden data analysis, file and application, and ownership.[9]

Time Frame Analysis

Every file is given a time and date stamp, which is updated every time that file is opened or modified. This is one reason why decisions regarding write blocking are so crucial. Windows and other file systems automatically check and update a number of files during the boot-up process. These processes are beyond user control and will render the access data invalid for future forensic analysis. The importance of temporal analysis should be clear in most cases. For example, time-date stamps could be helpful in proving that the suspect accessed a file or computer system several days after he stated he last logged in.

Hidden Data Analysis

This area of analysis includes cryptanalysis or and password cracking, steganalysis, and examination of data contained in the host protected area (HPA). We already have discussed cryptography and steganography, but the HPA is something you may not yet know about.

The HPA is a relatively new addition to hard drive architecture. It is an area of the disk that is allocated at the time of production so that manufacturers can include diagnostic software on the disk. Generally hidden from both the BIOS and the operating system, the HPA offers criminals a tidy place to hide important incriminating data.[10] Although there have been advances in the ability of forensic tools to identify HPA areas, they have been slow to provide tools for analysis and recovery of password-protected HPA disks. Several major players in the forensic tools game, including My Key Technologies, (www.MyKeyTech.com), Sanderson Forensics (www.sandersonforensics.co.uk), and Technology Pathways (www.techpathways.com), are working very hard in this area and have developed some tools to aid the forensic investigator in searching the HPA.

When analyzing hidden data, there are some things whose value is not quite so obvious as the evidentiary value of the information itself. These things, which I call metadata, can be very welcome additions to investigators' growing list of evidence. During password cracking and encryption analysis, recovery of the suspect's password might show more than just what is in the file. Password choices are usually very personal things, and often have some relationship to the person choosing them. The fact that an incriminating file is encrypted using a password that is also the suspect's daughter's name or birth date can be great circumstantial evidence.

Likewise, the very act of hiding data can be admissible evidence of knowledge of guilt. People do not usually hide things from public scrutiny without a reason. Hiding data, especially taking great measures such as restructuring a hard drive, hiding partitions, or falsely marking individual sectors as bad, is powerful evidence of a guilty mind. Investigators are always on the lookout for the metadata that might not be as obvious as the file containing the latest corporate trade secret.

Application and File Analysis

The actual analysis of each and every file on the suspect's system can take hundreds of hours. Yet it is often the only way to bring a case together. Investigators will be looking through the patent files—those not hidden from view—from a number of different angles.

First, investigators will be looking for patterns in the files. Date and time stamps can be valuable and might lead investigators to uncover the structure of the underlying scheme. Likewise, the appearance of particularly incriminating files may identify the exact date and time the offense occurs. Again, knowledge of the background on the case will inform an investigator's analysis.

For obvious reasons, investigators must examine the content of each file. Sometimes the files are exactly what they purport to be. Other times they are more heinous files masquerading as benign files. Child pornography and Trojan horse programs are two common examples of files whose outward appearance belies their true identity.

A number of programs are helpful to investigators conducting a file-by-file search. In addition to the viewing functions available in the forensic utility suites, stand-alone programs such as Quick View Plus (www.avantstar.com) from AvantStar Products give forensic technicians the ability to view almost any computer format available. Although Quick View Plus cannot necessarily open the file, it can guide investigators toward the correct file format or software program that can. In most cases, Quick View Plus can even recognize and view files whose extensions have been changed. If a suspect has changed an illegal image file's extension so that it appears to be an executable .bin file, for example, Quick View Plus will not be fooled.

Forensic examiners are also interested in the number and types of operating systems installed on the computer. While most operating systems support multiple boot configurations, such as a Windows XP partition and a Unix/Linux partition, not all users have the technical skill or the volition to take the extra time to create a dual-boot system. Often the existence of multiple operating systems can point to a computer user of greater skill than the average citizen. Again, this could be powerful evidence to counteract the suspect's claim that he is computer illiterate.

Visualizing the relationship between files and software on a computer system can also point investigators in new directions. If computer files that have no associated software are found on the disk, there may be other computer systems of interest to investigators, or perhaps the examiners missed something on the target computer, such as a hidden program or one that was recently deleted. Conversely, if investigators find a computer application—particularly one that should send up a red flag anyway, such as S-Tools (a steganography program)—and no associated files, then this could signal that further recovery efforts or steganalysis might be necessary.

Files that are always informative for investigators are the Internet history and cache files. Many times these files and their time-date stamps can provide a nearly day-by-day road map of the suspect's activities. The addresses and cached image files of hundreds or even thousands of Web sites may be lurking in this area, and careful scrutiny of their contents may lead to either the "smoking gun" or at least a strong shove toward that direction.

Ownership Analysis

Once the preceding steps have been completed, the process of assigning ownership to files and data on the computer should be complete. However, investigators often must look to a combination of the items discovered during earlier stages of the analysis process.

If investigators can find a way to place the offender in front of the computer at a particular time and date, it may be more likely to prove ownership or possession of the files in question. Likewise meta-analysis of things such as user-created files and unique file structures might help to establish that the suspect was in fact the person who placed the files on the computer.

As mentioned earlier, file name choices and passwords, also called pass phrases, may offer some very powerful clues as to ownership. File names that have a fairly unique relationship to the suspect, such as "Hanks file," might be all that investigators need to assign ownership. Likewise, the content of the files might offer some clues as to ownership. Valuable personal data commingled with contraband material could spell trouble for the suspect.

At the conclusion of the analysis, forensic examiners should have a pretty strong grasp of the case as a whole and the role the digital evidence plays. In drawing conclusions, forensic examiners must rely on a combination of experience, training, and a broad view of the evidence in its entirety. When taken in individual bites, the evidence may not lead to a particular conclusion; however, when looked at en masse, it can be surprisingly clear. Regardless of where the evidence in a particular examination points, the end result should be a better understanding of what processes and events were occurring on the suspect's computer and what the role of that computer was in the particular case under examination.

CONCLUSION

In this chapter, I have offered you a much more detailed look at the step-by-step process that computer forensic examiners go through when pursing an examination. It rarely matters whether examiners are looking for evidence to use in a criminal prosecution or a civil law-suit; the procedure rarely deviates much from the steps outlined in this chapter.

Using a combination of training, experience, and investigative ingenuity, computer forensic examiners comb through the bits and bytes of the hard drive, eventually distilling the raw data into something much more valuable to the investigation: evidence.

In the next chapter, I offer some insight into the legal dimensions that affect computer forensic professionals. Whether working in the civil arena or law enforcement, legal issues such as Fourth Amendment rights, freedom of speech, and even personal privacy all combine to create a landscape fraught with pitfalls and hidden traps. Regardless of your role in the computer forensic examination world, legal issues will impact the decisions you will make.

NOTES

1. Eoghan Casey, *Digital Evidence and Computer Crime: Forensic Science, Computers and the Internet* (Boston: Elsevier, 2004), p. 525. See also Christopher L. T. Brown, *Computer Evidence: Collection and Preservation* (Hingham, MA: Charles River Media, 2006), pp. 115–120.

2. Brown, *Computer Evidence,* p. 116.

3. Hooking is another way of saying that the high jacking code latches onto a very important system process, and then redirects its output to whatever the high-jacker chooses.

4. Ibid.

5. Bill Nelson, Amelia Phillips, Frank Enfinger, and Christopher Steuart, *Guide to Computer Forensics and Investigations,* 2nd ed. (Boston: Thomson Course Technology, 2006), p. 122. See also Brown, *Computer Evidence*, pp. 247–248.

6. See generally U.S. Department of Justice, *Forensic Examination of Digital Evidence: A Guide for Law Enforcement,* Office of Justice Programs, April 2004, p. 15.

7. Ibid.

8. Golden G. Richard III and Vassil Roussev, "Scalpel: A Frugal, High-Performance File Carver," Department of Computer Science, University of New Orleans. Available at: www.dfrws.org/2005/proceedings/richard_scalpel.pdf.

9. U.S. Department of Justice, *Forensic Examination.*

10. Brown, *Computer Evidence*, p. 145.

9

PRESENTING DIGITAL EVIDENCE IN COURT

INTRODUCTION

In the last chapter, we concluded our look at the process of examining a computer for digital evidence. Regardless of how thorough and precise forensic examiners are or how incriminating the evidence they find may be, the fact remains that the effort is wasted if certain legal hurdles have not been overcome. Likewise, the evidence will be no more than wasted time and money if the message gets lost in translation.

In this chapter, we discuss the nature of digital evidence that makes it different from many other forms of evidence. We also examine some of the fundamental basics of getting digital evidence into court.

When discussing the subject of computer forensics in the context of legal issues, the topics of Fourth Amendment protection and illegal search and seizure often dominate the conversation. Notwithstanding the fact that search and seizure

127

issues greatly impact the job of computer forensic professionals, our legal system influences the task in some other fundamental ways.

Whether collecting e-mails under electronic discovery or sifting through digital fragments of images on a child pornography case, nearly every aspect of the job of computer forensic technicians will be guided by the legal dimensions of the case and how it is to be presented to the end user. Sometimes the end user will be a superior; other times it may be a jury. In either case, the problems for computer forensic technicians will be the same—ensuring the message is received clearly and has as much impact as possible. To ensure this, technicians need to be aware of a number of things, some of which deal with presentation, others of which deal with the legal ramifications of the digital evidence seizure procedure.

EVIDENCE

All evidence can be broken down into two categories—circumstantial and direct. Of the two, direct evidence is probably the easiest to understand. Direct evidence is evidence that directly proves the fact that is in question. When I use the phrase "proves directly," I am referring to the fact that no intermediate steps are necessary to reach the conclusion. Direct evidence, then, might be thought of as the shortest distance to proving the fact. For example, eyewitness testimony of a robbery is considered direct evidence because a witness is testifying that she saw the defendant rob the store.[1]

Circumstantial evidence, however, is sometimes a bit tougher to get our heads around. Circumstantial evidence is evidence that is two or more steps removed from the ultimate fact. In the case of circumstantial evidence, the jury must make more than one step, which, unlike the situation with direct evidence, requires them to draw inferences. These inferences, as I discuss later, often make up the bulk of a case. As you might imagine, direct evidence would be ideal in all cases. If only we had an eyewitness to every crime. The reality is quite the opposite. Most cases are proven through circumstantial evidence.[2]

An example of circumstantial evidence would be testimony by a fingerprint expert that the defendant's fingerprints were found at the scene of the burglary. While tending to prove that the defendant was at the scene, it is not evidence directly showing that the defendant committed the burglary. In fact, there could be a number of reasons why the defendant's fingerprints were at the scene. Until the prosecutor successfully forges several more links in the chain of inferences, the conclusion that the defendant burglarized the house is not a reasonable one. To build the rest of this chain, the prosecutor will introduce more evidence, usually circumstantial, that both eliminate the possibility that the defendant's fingerprints were at the scene for legitimate reasons and tend to show that the defendant was the person who broke in.

Other items of circumstantial evidence might include a pawn ticket showing the defendant pawned the video-cassette recorder stolen from the house or witnesses who saw the defendant loitering in the area 20 minutes before the break-in. None of these links in the chain directly proves the ultimate fact the way our eyewitness to the robbery does, but, when taken as a whole, they add up to the conclusion that the defendant broke into the house.

TYPES OF EVIDENCE

Within the two categories of evidence, circumstantial and direct, there are different types. Based on the nature of the evidence, these types include real, testimonial, documentary, and demonstrative.[3]

Real evidence is sometimes called physical evidence. The term is used to describe physical things, such as guns, weapons, fingerprints, hair fibers, and other tangible things that the jury can touch, hold or feel.[4]

Testimonial evidence is the spoken word of a witness. People who witness the crime, those who testify to tests performed in a crime lab, and computer forensic experts who document the seizure and examination of digital evidence are providing testimonial evidence.[5]

Documentary evidence includes such obvious things as checks, bank statements, and written documents. In addition, it also includes such lesser-known things as computer printouts and computer logs. In short, documentary evidence may be thought of as a recorded writing that conveys a message.[6]

Demonstrative evidence is evidence that summarizes or explains other forms of evidence. Videotapes, films, charts, and graphs are all demonstrative evidence. Demonstrative evidence is often used to help testimonial witnesses further explain or clarify a complicated concept to which they are testifying. Computer forensic experts often rely on demonstrative evidence to help simplify the complicated computer evidence they are discussing.[7]

While it is entirely possible that computer forensic professionals will be called on for testimonial evidence, in reality, experts in computer forensics will be involved in all types of evidence, documentary, testimonial, real, and demonstrative. A computer forensic technician may need to render an expert opinion through testimony and also discuss the physical properties of the hard drive—real evidence. In order to do that, they may have to rely on an illustration—demonstrative exhibit—and computer printouts—documentary. As you can see, in this very simple scenario, one computer forensic expert has been called on to provide evidence in all four realms.

Nevertheless, the lion's share of what computer forensic experts will do falls under the heading of testimonial evidence. Therefore, we should discuss the different types of testimonial evidence.

There are generally two types of testimonial witnesses—lay witnesses and expert witnesses. Lay witnesses are sometimes referred to as fact witnesses. These witnesses testify to facts that are within their personal observation. Testimony that the suspect entered the store, drew a gun, and ordered the clerk to empty the register is layperson testimony. The witness, assuming he was in the store, personally observed the acts to which he is testifying. In most cases, the lay witness is the most common witness in the average trial (if such a thing exists).[8]

Expert witnesses have slightly greater latitude. They are allowed to testify to their opinions, provided that they are qualified in that field. Expert witness testimony is allowed in court because we believe that the expertise and experience of an expert witness in a particular area will help the judge and jury better understand a particular facet of the case.[9] Computer forensic experts are perfect examples of expert witnesses. Although the experts cannot render an opinion regarding the guilt or innocence of the defendant—that is the sole responsibility of the jury—they can offer an opinion as to particular elements of the offense. Experts hail from all facets of the scientific community and offer testimony on a variety of types of cases. It is entirely possible that an expert witness may also be used to testify as a lay witness, but rarely is it the other way around.

There is one exception to the rule that lay witnesses must testify only to observable facts. In some very limited circumstances, lay witnesses may be allowed to testify to opinions or conclusions drawn from inferences based on their perception. As long as the inferences will be helpful to the fact finder (jury) in reaching a decision about the fact in issue, the court may allow them.[10] A common example of this type of opinion testimony by a lay witness would be an opinion that the defendant was speeding or that the handwriting on a document was the defendant's handwriting.

Beyond this limited area, however, layperson testimony is strictly limited.

EXPERT WITNESSES

Because experts have such power in assisting the judge and jury, it is important that their testimony is reliable. To help ensure this reliability, certain rules have been put in place to help decide if and when expert witnesses can testify. These rules, designed to ensure that the jury does not improperly place too much weight on baseless opinions, focuses on two things: the field in which the witnesses will testify and the qualifications of the witnesses themselves. When preparing a case, prosecuting attorneys will carefully evaluate both.

This evaluation process generally occurs under what has become known as the *Daubert* test. The *Daubert* test is based on the landmark case of *Daubert v. Merrill Dow Pharmaceuticals,*[11] in which the Supreme Court rejected the previously used *Frye* test.[12] Under the *Frye* test, also known as the general acceptance test, the courts could exclude evidence that had not "gained general acceptance in the particular field in which it belongs."[13] The problems with the *Frye* test were many, but generally, most commentators viewed the test as too narrow and insufficient to deal with the fluid nature of scientific endeavors. In 1993, *Daubert* revolutionized the way the court system approached the question of scientific testimony and specifically addressed the admissibility of scientific expert testimony.

Under *Daubert,* the court established that scientific evidence is admissible if the

> expert is proposing to testify to (1) scientific knowledge that (2) will assist the trier of fact to understand or determine a fact in issue. This entails a preliminary assessment of whether the reasoning or methodology underlying the testimony is scientifically valid and of whether that reasoning or methodology properly can be applied to the fact in issue.[14]

While considering this case, the *Daubert* court referred to the role of the judiciary in such matters as the "gatekeeper" function and suggested that, while no checklist of admissibility should exist, courts use several factors as guideposts in determining whether scientific evidence should be admissible.[15] In *Daubert,* the court suggested these factors:

- Whether the theories and techniques employed by the scientific expert have been tested
- Whether the techniques employed by the expert have been subjected to peer review and publication

- Whether the techniques employed by the scientific expert have a known error rate
- Whether they are subject to standards governing their application
- Whether the theories and techniques employed by the expert enjoy widespread acceptance[16]

Considered a leap forward by many, the *Daubert* test has become the standard in both federal and state courts. In fact, Federal Rules of Evidence Rule 702 was amended in 2002 to incorporate the *Daubert* test as the threshold hurdle to the admissibility of scientific evidence. Most states have likewise adopted similar provisions in their own evidence codes.[17]

For several years under the *Daubert* test, evidence in all fields of scientific study had been uniformly evaluated and either admitted or excluded; however, as fields of study considered hybrids of scientific principle grew in popularity, concern arose over the applicability to *Daubert* to those areas. Simply put, the question arose whether *Daubert* governs scientific fields only or all field of expert testimony. Fields such as engineering and perhaps even computer forensics, although based in the scientific fields of physics and mathematics, are very technical as well. In order to clear up any confusion over which fields *Daubert* should apply to, the Supreme Court clarified the issue in *Kumho Tire Co. v. Carmichael*.[18]

In the *Kumho* decision, the Court extended the *Daubert* factors to all cases in which expert testimony is rendered, as long as the testimony was based on "specialized knowledge."[19] This case necessarily encompasses computer forensics and therefore is very important in this field. Likewise, it has unified a number of issues and makes admissibility of expert testimony easier to plan for. Assuming the expert's qualifications are acceptable, and the field meets the *Daubert/Kumho* test, the evidence, if relevant, will be admissible to help the court and jury reach a verdict.

While I glossed over the term "relevant," it is important to touch on the role that relevance plays in questions of evidence admissibility.

LEGAL REQUIREMENTS OF EVIDENCE

As I indicated, a case is rarely proven in a court of law with one single piece of evidence. Instead, the prosecutor or plaintiff slowly builds the case using a number of intermediate steps along the way. These intermediate steps are the inferences. Some inferences are clear, while others require a bit more effort on the part of the audience. The goal of the prosecutor is to make the effort required by the audience as low as possible. These inferences can also be thought of as the steps on a bridge across a deep gorge. If point A on one side of the gorge is 200 feet from point B on the other side of the gorge, a traveler moving from point A to B will need some steps on the bridge to get there. If we think of these steps as inferences in our chain of proof, fewer inferences mean bigger steps since there will be greater distance between each step. In the case of proving complicated cases, baby steps are often preferable since they require smaller steps, taking the jury one little step at a time.

Building one inference on another, the prosecutor carefully places the step on the bridge. Thus, the bridge, when completed, will carry the jury to the conclusion that the defendant is guilty. In the legal world, these steps, or chains of inferences, form the heart of nearly every case. With large distances between the steps, a successful prosecution is unlikely.

The prosecutor must therefore make sure that every step is as strong as the next. The testimony of computer forensic experts forms one or several of the steps across the bridge in an average digital case. Ensuring the strength of these individual steps is not always an easy task. Failure of these steps can occur either because the evidence is inadmissible or because the witness's presentation was faulty.

Of all the requirements placed on evidence, the most well known is probably relevance. Any time parties to a legal action seeks to introduce evidence, whether digital or otherwise, there must be a connection between the evidence that they are seeking to put before the jury and the cause of action before it; we call this relevance. In some cases relevance is fairly apparent at the outset; at other times it may be more obtuse.

In layman's terms, relevant evidence can be defined as any evidence that tends to prove or disprove any material fact in dispute.[20] Sometimes, the fact that is in dispute is the ultimate question of guilt or innocence. Most times, however, the fact in question is only *related* to that ultimate fact in issue. For example, testimony of an eyewitness that he personally saw the defendant break into the computer system would be relevant to the question of guilt or innocence. The relevance here is quite clear. The testimony of a digital forensic technician that the defendant's computer had a password cracking program installed would also be relevant, but in a less obvious way.

Although the latter testimony does not prove the ultimate fact, it does prove an inferior fact that makes it more or less likely that the defendant committed the act in question. As you can see, the farther away from the ultimate fact, guilt or innocence, we move, the less clear relevance becomes. In fact, when trying to build a long chain of inferences leading up to an ultimate conclusion, prosecutors often seek to introduce evidence that at first glance appears to have no relevance whatsoever.

If a prosecutor attempted to enter a defendant's first-year college class schedule into evidence in a prosecution for a computer trespass that occurred 12 years later, the relevance may not immediately become clear. However, if we also know that the courses the defendant took during that year involved programming the very same type of computer system he is accused of breaking into, the relevance become clear. Although taking a computer programming course in college does not prove he broke into the computer system—the ultimate fact in question—it does prove a link in the chain of inferences. That link in this case would be that the defendant was familiar with and possessed the skills necessary to commit the crime.

As you might guess, what becomes relevant evidence is based largely on which chain of inferences the prosecutor is trying to establish. Like life itself, there are often a number of different routes by which you can reach a particular destination. Legal proof is similar in that there are often several theories of the case through which attorneys can seek to prove their case. Depending on which theory attorneys select as their strongest attack point, the definition of what is relevant evidence may change.

Now that we understand a little bit more about both relevance and the rules governing when experts can testify in a case, let us look at some of the other rules that relate to the admission of evidence. First, we turn to the chain of custody.

The chain of custody rule is another way in which courts try to ensure that evidence is reliable. According to this rule, all persons who could have tampered with, substituted, or contaminated evidence must be documented.[21] If the chain of custody is improperly documented or does not exist, evidence admissibility is doubtful. The net effect of this requirement is that every piece of evidence must be traced from the point it is collected until the point at which it is introduced as evidence. This tracking is done through evidence receipts, sealed containers, and officer testimony. Items such as videotapes, photographs, drugs, and bullets have all been held to this requirement, as have semen, blood, and, of course, digital evidence.

In the digital world, part of the chain of custody documentation can be the hash values discussed in Chapter 8. Because the hash value is a unique and scientifically reliable way to identify a file and prove that alteration has not taken place, it is a powerful tool for proving that the item that was seized and introduced into evidence has not been tampered with or altered.

Other problems that computer forensic investigators face in terms of chain of custody involve the very nature of digital evidence itself. As we discussed in earlier chapters, the very act of observation in the digital world—moving a mouse or browsing the web—changes values in the evidence. If computer forensic technicians seize a hard drive and then begin exploring the files, regardless of whether they intentionally alter anything, the evidence they will present in court will not be the same evidence that was seized. Of course, these rules are subject to certain limitations; however, computer forensic investigators are always cognizant of the unique problems chain of custody can inject into digital forensic cases.

In addition to chain of custody concerns, prosecutors must be aware of the best evidence rule. The best evidence rule applies to writings, documents, recordings, photographs, and, of course, certain forms of digital evidence, with some slight variation.[22] The rule requires attorneys to place into evidence only original documents, tapes, and so on. There are certain exceptions to these rules, however, such as when the original is no longer available, unless there is a genuine question regarding the authenticity of the duplicate. In addition, the rule is rather liberal when defining "original." For example, each photograph made from a single negative is considered an original. In the computer realm, this definition can be helpful.

Since true digital evidence is unreadable by human eyes, the best evidence rule would seem to preclude any admissibility of anything other than the actual 0s and 1s in their original form. Luckily, the rules of evidence are not so rigid as to work this injustice. Like photographs, the courts consider printouts and images derived from computer data to be originals for the purpose of the best evidence rule. In other words, assuming there is no question regarding the underlying data, printouts and computer-generated images should be readily admissible under this rule.

Last in our discussion of admissibility, we should discuss hearsay. Hearsay is loosely defined as any statement, other than a statement made in court, that is offered into evidence to prove the truth of the matter asserted.[23] Although the definition of hearsay gives my students and most first-year law students fits, it is really quite simple in concept. As I explained earlier, reliability is the linchpin of our rules of evidence. Reliability can be assured in several ways—chain of custody and the best evidence rules are just two of them. These rules deal with real evidence—items whose veracity can be measured in finite terms. Either the evidence has been altered or it has not. Testimonial evidence is another matter entirely.

In our legal system, the greatest tool to show the reliability of testimonial evidence is the act of cross-examination. It is through cross-examination that opposing attorneys can probe the limits of the witness's veracity and establish that the testimony is less than reliable. Without this power of cross-examination, the opponent is left nearly powerless to defend him- or herself. The rules about hearsay come to the rescue. Hearsay rules are designed to prevent unassailable testimony from coming into court because it cannot be subjected to the "trial by fire" of cross-examination. This is all well and good; however, the waters usually get muddier when we begin to discuss the exceptions to the hearsay exclusion rules.

Without going into too much detail I must explain that a number of exceptions allow certain out-of-court statements to come into court. Close examination of each and every exception reveals a logical reason for its existence, based on reliability. I will not illustrate each exception, just give an example based on one of the more common exceptions: the excited utterance.

An excited utterance is a spontaneous statement that a person makes that is of some relevance to the case. Perhaps the person screams "Oh no, it's John, and he has a gun." Under normal circumstances, the prosecutor would subpoena the witness who saw John with the gun; she would take the stand and recount what she saw. However, if the witness is no longer available—perhaps she died—then her statement is hearsay and could be subject to exclusion—if not for the excited utterance exception.

This exception allows statements made under the pressure and stress of the event and without time for studied reflection into court—even though they are hearsay by definition. The reason is clear if we think in terms of reliability.[24]

Since statements made without the ability to attack them are by nature unreliable, we need to look for some other reason for believe their truth. In this case, as a society, we believe that people who are under the pressure of a stressful event, who do not have time to scheme, will utter the truth. So, in this case, the circumstances surrounding the statement lead us to believe the statement is reliable in its own right. It becomes sort of self-proving.

Similar logic underpins all our exceptions to the hearsay rule, such as dying declarations. As a society, we believe that people who are dying will be honest for fear of meeting their maker with a lie on their lips. Thus, their dying words are admissible even though they are hearsay.

This hearsay problem becomes a computer forensic problem because the courts have expanded hearsay to include nonverbal communications and documents. Using our rudimentary knowledge of hearsay, that should cause us some concerns when we begin contemplating entering computer documents into evidence.

Have no fear; our exceptions will pave the way. Another hearsay exception is the business records exception. Most courts have allowed the introduction of computer records, including investigative records of forensic computer analysts, into court under this exception.[25] Under this exception, records kept in the regularly conducted activity of a business are allowed into evidence regardless of whether the maker is available in court or not. While the courts have routinely applied this rule to any number of business records, from accounting records to personnel records, they have recently expanded the scope to include computer records as well.

As you can see, the rules that govern when evidence can be used in legal proceedings can be quite complicated. If practitioners are careless about chain of custody or documenting the seizure and collection of digital evidence, all the hard work may be for naught. Yet even if computer forensic technicians are careful in their methods and meticulous in their documentation, there are other land mines that can spell trouble. These land mines usually are related to the Fourth Amendment.

SEARCH AND SEIZURE

The Fourth Amendment protects citizens only from government action. Therefore, one of the first questions constitutional law students are trained to ask is "Where is the state action?" If the response to that question is "There is none," then no Fourth Amendment violation has occurred. The simplicity of that example belies the fact that answering the first question can be unbelievably complicated, especially in situations that are blended, such as the quasi-government agencies and government agencies acting in their administrative capacity. Regardless, the fact remains that where no state action exists, there is no violation of a citizen's rights under the Fourth Amendment.

For computer forensic investigators, this fact usually means that when the engagement for which they were hired is strictly administrative or civil in nature, there will be little need to be cognizant of the protections afforded defendants under the Fourth Amendment. However, that does not absolve investigators from all liability. Even where constitutional protections leave off, civil remedies are available, such as trespass, defamation, invasion of privacy, and malicious prosecution.

The only protection the Fourth Amendment affords is against illegally seized evidence from being used in a criminal prosecution. Like all rules, this rule, known as the exclusionary rule, has exceptions. Notwithstanding the exceptions, it holds that any evidence that agents of the government seize in violation of a citizen's Fourth Amendment right must be excluded from court.[26] Many motions to suppress have been fought over what the parameters of this rule are, and volumes of law texts fill our legal libraries expounding on the propriety of such a rule. Regardless of whether the rule is good or bad for society, it is the rule law enforcement must be cognizant of when investigating all crimes—including computer crimes. Likewise, private computer forensic technicians, when working at the request of a law enforcement agency, are agents of the police and therefore must follow the Fourth Amendment's strictures just like the agency itself.

The Fourth Amendment's two greatest requirements are that police have "probable cause" to search and that they have a warrant. Distilling these two very complicated requirements into the space of an entire book, let alone a few paragraphs, would be difficult. Therefore, please forgive me if the abridged version of these requirements provides only a glancing explanation.

Probable cause is simply enough evidence to cause a reasonable person in the officer's position to believe that evidence of a crime exists in the place to be searched.[27] Courts have wrestled with this definition for many years, and it varies slightly from jurisdiction to jurisdiction; however, the fundamental tenets remain the same. Officers must have evidence, not a mere hunch, but that evidence need not be nearly the level of evidence to warrant a conviction. For example, many experts equate probable cause to a numeric value of 51 percent.[28]

The requirement of a reasonable person in the officer's position is designed to recognize that trained and experienced police officers are likely to view a collection of disparate facts in a light very different from that of an untrained person. Police officers develop their experience over time, and part of this experience allows them to draw conclusions that the rest of the world might not make, simply because they do not have the same level of expertise in the area. When combined together, these elements constitute the probable cause requirement that must be present in nearly all police searches. The probable cause requirement is the same in the computer venue as in the nondigital world: Police must have probable cause to search for digital evidence.

The second prong, the warrant requirement, is sometimes seen as a more flexible requirement. Over time, it has developed a rather lengthy list of exceptions.[29] Rather than list the exceptions, it would be simpler to explain the rationale for them. Generally, the courts have carved out exceptions where exigencies exist. These exigencies generally center on things such as destruction of evidence or perhaps destruction of life. The exigencies are then balanced against the reason for the warrant requirement in the first place.

The warrant requirement was instituted largely to combat discretionary searches, without prior review. Today's requirement that a neutral party review the probable cause the police officers claim to have acts as a protection against officers' indiscriminate searches supported by probable cause developed "after the fact." The belief is that if, before they are allowed to search, officers are required to tell a neutral party what facts and circumstances are known to them that lead them to believe that probable cause exists, fewer abusive searches will occur. Although this is true, the exceptions usually address those situations in which circumstances make getting a warrant highly impractical. Remember, the warrant exceptions do not do away with the probable cause requirement; they simply move the point in time when neutral parties review the probable cause to later.

These fundamental rules are part of the constitutional guarantees our founding fathers viewed as being so essential that they have become part of our legal legacy. While they are clearly powerful constraints on the power of the state, they fall short. To compensate for some of the shortcomings inherent in such broad and sweeping legal rules, the government has created laws to help enforce and supplement the Fourth Amendment. Although the number and scope of these laws would fill a small library, a few are of particular importance to computer forensic investigators.

The first is the Wiretap Act. Although police have been collecting evidence of criminal wrongdoing for years using wire intercepts, the advent of computer technology threw a curveball at them. The Wiretap Act, also known as Title III, protects citizens from the police tapping their phone lines without prior court authorization.[30] Acting as a statutory enactment of the Fourth Amendment protection against unlawful searches and seizures, Title III requires that police obtain a judge's written approval for their application to tap a phone. This application must contain facts and circumstances that lead a reasonable person to believe that evidence of a crime will be obtained by listening to the suspect's telephone conversations.

A tremendously difficult order to obtain, a Title III intercept has historically been reserved for major federal cases involving things such as organized crime and narcotics. However, as computers emerged, new problems developed, including exactly what constituted a wiretap under Title III.

For example, sending e-mail over the Internet is a communication sent by wire, and some interpretations of Title III would include intercepting an e-mail message under its purview. Others however do not. As the ambiguity grew, so did the realization that e-mails, although sharing some similarities to telephone conversations, also are very different from them.

For one thing, telephone networks operate on a circuit-switching basis. In other words, telephones connect to one another in a direct closed circuit that exists as long as the circuit is complete. E-mail communications travel in a packet-switched environment. What this means is that e-mails are broken into packets and delivered in small pieces, using any available node, to get to their final destination, where they are reassembled. A telephone call has one single continuous route. E-mails have many different paths to the same destination.[31]

This difference, combined with a number of other problems, necessitated some changes in the way the law deals with digital information. Thus, the Electronic Communications Privacy Act (ECPA) was born.[32] This act, which is essentially an amendment to Title III, specifically addresses the problems inherent in computer and other electronic communications. One change is in the way we view the communications themselves.

In brief, the ECPA seeks to categorize the privacy interests in electronic communications. In doing so, it requires investigators to classify several aspects of each electronic communication before they can determine what procedure is necessary to legally seize information. The first classification relates to the provider of the networking service. Next investigators must decide whether the communication is a stored electronic communication or other information, such as account subscriber information. Last they must decide if the information is being compelled by the state—for example, under court order. Answers to these questions will determine which avenue investigators must pursue.

While the nuances of this complex amendment are well beyond the scope of this book, the rules governing whether the government investigator needs a warrant or court order or a Title III intercept order are topics all investigators should become familiar with. If issues that point toward the ECPA arise, careful reading of the ECPA itself and close consultation with legal counsel are crucial in order to steer clear of land mines. Lest computer forensic investigators who are working for private individuals or on civil cases believe they are safe, they must think again. The ECPA and Title III also apply to nongovernmental entities in certain circumstances and can provide for hefty civil fines upon conviction.[33]

Based on an analysis under the Fourth Amendment, Title III, and the ECPA, investigators will usually determine that there are one or more of three options for evidence recovery.

The first option is consent. Title III, the ECPA, and most state statutory equivalents provide for voluntary release of information. However, consent in this case may not be clear cut. Consent must be given by a party with authorization. For example, in some circumstances, a computer system administrator whose system has been hacked may give consent. This situation may arise when the hacker is still in the system and actively attacking the administrator's system. In that case, a system administrator may be able to authorize an active intercept. In other cases, however, the system administrator may not have the authority to consent. In some court cases, it has been held that where the system administrator's system is merely a leapfrog point for connection to a third computer, there is a question as to the administrator's ability to consent under the ECPA.[34]

Additionally, investigators may place some confidence in banners, those bothersome welcome screens that most computer systems now require users to acknowledge in order to use the system. If they are properly worded and clearly put users on notice that by entering the site they are consenting to monitoring of their activities, these banners constitute consent to monitor later on.[35]

Next in order of complexity is the search warrant. A search warrant to seize computer evidence is really no more difficult to secure than a search warrant for nondigital evidence. The difficulty often lies in the warrant preparation and the execution. Search warrants always require a formal application with a supporting affidavit outlining the facts and circumstances that establish probable cause. Digital evidence warrants are no different. However, those who prepare the affidavit and the listing of items to be searched and seized must be fairly computer savvy.

Last, and perhaps the most daunting of all, is the actual intercept of communications. In the nondigital world, the interception of communications occurs under Title III. This process is very technically complex and requires a tremendous amount of manpower to effectively minimize the information that is collected. For example, Title III intercepts require that agents exclude any and all communications unrelated to the case or for which no probable cause exists. This requirement means that the intercept must be monitored 24/7 and conversations must be surgically spliced in real time—a difficult undertaking in the best of circumstances and very time and labor intensive. Add multilingual suspects and the problems quadruple. In the digital world, the complexity of intercepts is greatly reduced.

Although the same minimization requirement is present, the technology of electronic communications makes tasks such as this child's play. Computer technology and filtering devices make collection of only that network traffic that pertains to the order an automated and nearly hands-off process. Likewise, integration of the law enforcement technology with the service provider's technology is usually a simple matter—something that is often not the case in traditional Title III intercepts.

While on the subject of an intercept, it is appropriate to mention the Carnivore program, a computer program developed by the FBI that serves as an intercept device.[36] Among Carnivore's talents is the ability to sniff out network traffic and extract all communications related to the target. Carnivore intercepts and records these packets before they are passed along to their final destination. The power of Carnivore is mind-boggling, and it has rightly given rise to claims of overzealousness on the part of the government. Regardless of Carnivore's power, the fact remains that government deployment of the program is still subject to the rules and limitations of the Fourth Amendment and all subsequent legislation supporting it.

Another area of high-tech surveillance that has garnered both legal and public scrutiny is the real-time monitoring of data terminals. Called keystroke monitoring, this practice collects every single key press and mouse click a user makes on a computer system.[37] This method of employee monitoring, which appears oppressive to some, is viewed by others as a legitimate right of employers. Given the reduced expectation of privacy that most employees have, especially when using their employers' resources, it is not surprising that courts routinely uphold the employer rights to monitor employee behavior in such a way.

What is perhaps more surprising is that the courts have allowed law enforcement some latitude as well. In fact, the courts appear to be prepared to draw a line—arbitrary, some would say—at the modem cable. In the note-worthy case of *U.S. v. Scarfo,* the U.S. District Court for the Southern District of New Jersey upheld a keylogging intercept of Nicodemo Scarfo's computer activities.[38] The FBI, while investigating Scarfo for federal bookmaking and loan-sharking violations, installed a keystroke logger on his computer. When Scarfo was on the computer but not connected to the Internet, the agents would log all his computer activity and review it. When Scarfo was on the Internet, the agents did not monitor. Using the information they obtained when monitoring Scarfo's computer activity, they obtained an indictment and subsequent conviction.[39] The court found that the government's actions in the case did not violate the Wiretap Act, since they were not intercepting a wire communication.

CONCLUSION

Computer technology influences all aspects of our lives. Nowhere perhaps is this more evident than in our legal system, where courts must help us define the boundaries of acceptable and unacceptable behavior. In the world of computers, this process can be greatly complicated due to the fact that many players in the system lack a true grasp of the fundamental nature of the digital world. There are both similarities and differences between the digital and the nondigital world. The task of the legal community, with the assistance of the technical community, is to sort out which of these differences are important enough to warrant changes in the way we view evidence. Likewise, computer experts must help guide us in deciding which similarities are truly similarities or merely appear to be so at first glance.

Without the guidance of trained technology professionals, the legal professionals who are in charge of helping us establish boundaries will be left with very little guidance. The resulting hodge-podge of laws will create a legal landscape cluttered with insurmountable mountains and deadly precipices into which practitioners such as computer forensic professionals and law enforcement investigators will fall headlong. Using a combination of technical expertise and legal know-how, our legal system will slowly evolve into a digital-savvy world where the rules are much clearer and the path is well paved. Until that time, it is important for computer forensic professionals to use common sense, good judgment, and frequent consultation with legal counsel as they carefully pick their way through the digital world.

NOTES

1. Charles P. Nemeth, *Law and Evidence: A Primer for Criminal Justice, Criminology, Law, and Legal Studies* (Upper Saddle River, NJ: Prentice-Hall, 2001), p. 15.
2. Ibid.
3. See generally ibid.
4. Ibid., pp. 31–41.
5. Ibid., pp. 15–16.
6. Ibid., p. 20.
7. Ibid., pp. 71–74.
8. Ibid., pp. 151–169.
9. Ibid., pp. 173–174.
10. Ibid., p. 155.
11. 509 U.S. 579 (1993).
12. *Frye v. United States,* 293 Fed.1013 (D.C. Cir. 1923).
13. Ibid.
14. Hamilton, "The Movement from Frye to Daubert: Where Do the States Stand," *Jurimetrics Journal* 38 (1998): 201.
15. *Daubert,* 509 U.S. at 590
16. Ibid. at 593.
17. T. J. Gardner and T. M. Anderson, *Criminal Evidence: Principles and Cases,* 6th ed. (Belmont, CA: Thomson Wadsworth, 2007), p. 377.
18. 119 S. Ct. 37, 142.
19. Ibid.
20. Nemeth, *Law and Evidence,* pp. 6–9.

21. Ibid., p. 56.
22. Gardner and Anderson, *Criminal Evidence,* p. 364.
23. Nemeth, *Law and Evidence,* 140.
24. Ibid., p. 24.
25. See *United States v. Cestnik,* 36 F.3d 904, 909–10 (10th Cir. 1994); *United States v. Moore,* 923 F.2d 910, 914 (1st Cir. 1991); *United States v. Briscoe,* 896 F.2d 1476, 1494 (7th Cir. 1988); *United States v. Catabran,* 836 F.2d 453, 457 (9th Cir. 1988).
26. Gardner and Anderson, *Criminal Evidence,* p. 168.
27. John N. Ferdico, *Criminal Procedure for the Criminal Justice Professional,* 9th ed. (Belmont, CA: Thomson Wadsworth, 2005), pp. 110–113.
28. Ibid.
29. Ibid., pp. 210–213.
30. 18 U.S.C. Sections 2510–22.
31. Christos J. Moschovitis, Hilary Poole, Tami Schuyler, and Theresa M. Senft, *History of the Internet: A Chronology, 1843 to the Present* (Santa Barbara, CA: ABC-CLIO, 1999), pp. 45–46.
32. 18 U.S.C. Sections 2701–10.
33. Ibid.
34. Robert Strang, "Recognizing and Meeting Title III Concerns in Computer Investigations" (Washington, DC: U.S. Department of Justice, March 2001).
35. Ibid.
36. John Vacca, *Computer Forensics: Computer Crime Scene Investigation* (Hingham, MA: Charles River Media, 2002), pp. 448–451.
37. Ibid., pp. 472–473.
38. *United States v. Scarfo et al.,* 180 F. Supp 2d 572 (2001).
39. Ibid.

INDEX